# A Rustling
# *of* Wings

## An Angelic Guide
## to the Twin Cities

JOAN NYBERG

1994
·Wingtip·Press·
St. Paul

The views expressed in this book are those of the author, and do not necessarily represent the beliefs of the churches, individuals or organizations named herein.

Every effort has been made to ensure that the information in this book was accurate at the time of publication. The author and publisher assume no responsibility for errors, inaccuracies, omissions or any other inconsistencies. Any perceived slights against people or organizations are unintentional.

The author gratefully acknowledges Kathleen Priest for granting permission to reproduce "Angel with Bass," copyright 1990; and Carolyn Miller, for permission to use "Realm of Possiblity."

Library of Congress Catalog Card Number: 94-90051

ISBN 0-9640578-2-4

Printed in the United States of America.

First printing, June 1994
Second printing, February 1995, revised

Book design: Judy Gilats, Peregrine Graphics Services
Cover design: Black Dog Graphics
Cover photo: Richard Nyberg, *Sacristy dome angel, Cathedral of St. Paul.*

*In loving memory of*
*Grams,*
*Helen Caroline Holland*
*(1899–1976),*
*who knew about joy.*

## Acknowledgments

First, I'd like to thank God and the angels for their guidance and inspiration. A special, heart-felt thanks is due my husband, Richard. He not only took most of the photographs, but also supported and encouraged me throughout the book's creation. Thank you to our son, Peter, for his patience on our angel-scouting expeditions. (He's the only four year old I know who knows the archangels by name.)

The book wouldn't have happened without the support of my sister, Ann, who believed in me and in the project even when I didn't. Thanks also to the rest of my family, Mom, Mary, David, Toni, Kaitrin, Olivia, Avis, Carol and Lee. The editing of Bonnie Anderson, Sue O'Donnell and Antona Richardson improved the manuscript tremendously. And the friendship of Mary Bisbee, Barbara Garland, Diane Richardson, Marcy Shilling and many others saw me through the rough patches along the way.

I am indebted to Judy Gilats, who shepherded the book through the production phase. I'd also like to acknowledge John Salisbury and John Wall, who steered me toward many local angel images; the people who contributed their personal stories or art works to this book; and the clergy and staff members of the many churches I visited.

# Contents

## REALM OF POSSIBILITY

They might
be there, just
out of sight, rustling
faintly, almost
touching us:
the bemused,
slightly puzzled
angels, wanting
us to be happy.

*Carolyn Miller*

# PREFACE

THIS BOOK BEGAN with a cup of coffee and a prayer. Exhausted from holiday preparations, I downed a cup of French roast on Christmas Eve, about noontime. I needed a jolt to make it through the day. Tired as I felt, I was sure I'd be able to sleep that night, despite the caffeine.

Eleven hours and two Christmas celebrations later, I realized I'd underestimated caffeine's powerful effect on me once again. With no hope of sleep in sight, I decided to while away some wakeful hours attending midnight mass at a neighborhood church—not one I attend regularly.

I arrived early. The musicians were tuning up in the choir loft and just a half dozen people sat in the wooden pews below. Settling in, I pulled out a notebook and began jotting down a few thoughts about the season and my hopes for the coming year.

One of my wishes for the new year, along with health, happiness and 10 fewer pounds, was for more joy in my work. A freelance writer, I write for local corporations—mainly brochures and stories for employee publications. It's interesting work, but I felt the need for a change.

Putting away my notebook, I looked around the sanctuary,

surprised to see so many angels there—in the windows, on the altar, everywhere. Though I'd visited the church before, I hadn't noticed the angels.

My interest in angels began about a decade ago, during the holidays. I had a strong, persistent feeling that there was something I needed to buy for the people on my Christmas list. I didn't know what it was, but I was certain I'd recognize it when I found it. (Try telling that to the shoppers' assistants at department stores!) When I stumbled across some wooden angel ornaments, carved in Germany, I knew I'd found what I was searching for: angels.

Every Christmas season since, I've felt compelled to look for angels. I send angel Chrsitmas cards, give angel gifts, make angel cookies and decorate my tree and home with angels. Over the years, I started thinking of angels as more than a decorative image. I began to feel their loving, guiding, protecting presence in my life.

I don't see miraculous apparitions of angels in all their winged glory, though I don't doubt that some people do. The angels come to me in more subtle ways. In fortunate "coincidences" and heightened intuition, I hear the rustling of wings.

After the last chorus of "Joy to the World," I walked home through the swirling snow in the first few moments of that Christmas morning. As I slept that night, the music, the angels, the sparkling snow, the celebration of Christ's birth and the prayer for joy all danced in my head instead of sugarplums. The idea for this book came the next morning, like a special gift left under the tree.

The answer to a Christmas prayer, this book has given me tremendous joy. It's put me in touch with some extraordinary people and places I never would have encountered otherwise. My hope is that this book is received in the spirit in which it was written, and that the joy and love I've felt in creating it come through to you, no matter how you view the angels.

People hold widely differing ideas about angels, from complete disinterest to skepticism to wild enthusiasm. Some believe angels are merely an interesting image that dates back centuries. Some put strict limits on what angels are and who they'll help. Many people believe angels are active in their lives right now. Some even claim to speak with angels regularly.

I don't believe there is one correct view of the angels or one correct way to experience their presence, but I do know this: Angels are for everyone. They are there for us, whether we believe in them or not. The more open we become to the angels, the more active and helpful they can become in our lives.

How do you become "open" to angels? There are many ways. Prayer and meditation are perhaps the most evident. You can also try drawing or painting angels, singing about them, reading books about them, attending angel seminars or just looking at beautiful images of angels.

Here in the Twin Cities, we are blessed with a wealth of angel representations. From places of worship and museums to cemetery chapels and retail shops, angels are all around us. This book guides you to the angels in our midst.

# ALL ABOUT ANGELS

IT'S NOT MY intention to present a complete angelology, or study of angels. Volumes have been written on the subject. Yet it helps to have a little understanding of the angelic tradition before setting off to see angels.

Judaism, Christianity and Islam are the three major religions that acknowledge angels, though nearly all world religions recognize beings that perform angel-like functions. Spirits that serve as intermediaries between humans and the divine exist in Asian, Native American and African traditions among others.

Angels appear 43 times in Christian and Hebrew scriptures and are mentioned more than 200 times in the Bible.

The word angel comes from the Greek word *angelos,* meaning messenger, which itself is a translation of the Hebrew word for messenger, *mal'ak.*

In the Bible, angels frequently function as messengers between God and humans. Three angels visited Abraham and gave him some surprising news: His aging wife, Sarah, would bear him a son, despite her years. (It may have been this angel visit Paul had in mind when he wrote, "Be not forgetful to entertain strangers: For thereby some have entertained angels unawares." Hebrews 13:2)

The Archangel Gabriel appeared to Mary and delivered the message that she was to become the mother of Jesus. An angel appeared to Joseph in a dream, telling him not to be afraid to take Mary as his wife, for she was pregnant by the Holy Spirit. Another angel told Joseph to take Mary and the baby Jesus into Egypt, for Herod sought to destroy the child. On the first Easter morning, an angel addressed a group of women, who were surprised to find Jesus' tomb empty. "He is not here," the angel told them. "He is risen." Important messages, all.

In the Bible and in accounts of human-angel experiences, angels bring us two messages again and again: Fear not, and praise God always.

Yet angels are more than mere messengers. They serve many purposes. They protect, defend, comfort, heal, guide, liberate, praise, sing, adore and offer good counsel. They bring peace, acceptance, understanding and laughter. They worship God constantly.

Some say that angels are God's thoughts, everywhere at once, attending to even the smallest details of existence. How different our world would be if our own thoughts were so beautiful: robed in radiant light, expressing love and inspiring peace wherever they appear.

I sometimes like to think of angels as manifestations of God and his love for us. It's not a terribly original idea. The concept dates back to Zoroaster (628–551 B.C.), founder of an ancient Persian religion.

Angels are divine beings in the sense that they are "of God," but they are not God. They are not to be worshipped. Revelation 22:8–9 makes clear that all praise is due to God, not to the angels. "I fell down to worship before the feet of the angel which showed me these things. Then saith he unto me, See thou do it not: for I am thy fellow servant . . . worship God."

There's a difference between worshipping an angel and just being polite. I believe it's perfectly fine to pray to the angels, asking for their assistance and thanking them for their help. To cover all the bases, say, "Thank you God. Thank you angels," for the blessings you receive.

## Angel Images

Many experts believe the earliest representation of an angel dates back to the Sumerians of Babylon (4000–1000 B.C.). Images of winged spirits can also be found in the ancient cultures of Mesopotamia, Egypt and Greece.

Angels rarely appeared in early Christian art until after the time of Constantine I, who ruled the Roman empire from 306 to 337 A.D. Artists didn't want to risk comparison to the winged gods of Greece and Rome. Even then, angels were only pictured when they played a central role in the Bible story being illustrated, such as Gabriel's appearance to Mary at the Annunciation.

By the fifth century, angels were used with abandon, no longer limited to their documented appearances in the Bible. They were often shown as attendants, praising or waiting on Jesus or Mary.

Though angels in the Bible are either male or genderless, angels took on a very feminine feel during the late Middle Ages and especially during the Renaissance. During this period, something curious also happened to the powerful, towering cherubim, who guarded the gates to Eden and protected the palaces of ancient Mesopotamia. These figures of power and protection were some-how transformed into "putti," or cherubs, sweet baby angels that flit about in their chubby altogether.

In her book, "Touched by Angels," Eileen Elias Freeman says

childlike angels began appearing in art in the late Middle Ages, when many infants and young children died in the plagues. Their grief-stricken parents were comforted by the thought that their "little angels" were now in heaven. (She clearly points out, however, that humans don't become angels when they die.)

## The Angelic Hierarchy

According to Pseudo-Dionysius, Thomas Aquinas, Pope Gregory and others, there are nine choirs or gradations of angels in the angelic hierarchy, each with different responsibilities to God and humankind. The nine choirs encircle the throne of God, each in its own "orbit." From closest to furthest from God, the following are the nine choirs.

1. Seraphim stand at the throne of God, ceaselessly singing "Holy, Holy Holy." Their song is an act of creation and celebration, of life and love. It was the six-winged seraphim that the prophet Isaiah saw above the throne of God.

2. Cherubim are keepers of knowledge and wisdom. God stationed the mighty cherubim east of Eden to guard the way to the tree of life. The prophet Ezekiel spied four cherubim, each with four faces and four wings.

3. Thrones are also known as ophanim, galgallin or wheels. The thrones are the fiery wheels that Ezekiel described (Ezekiel 1:13–19). They bring justice to humankind.

4. Dominations, or dominions, regulate angels' duties and serve as channels of mercy.

5.  Virtues work miracles on earth, through the power of God. They offer courage and grace to humans.

6.  Powers defend the world against demons and keep the physical laws of the universe in good working order.

7.  Principalities, sometimes called princes, are protectors of religion. They protect good spirits from attacks by evil ones.

8.  Archangels are messengers that carry divine decrees, and serve as guardians of people and physical things. The seven angels that stand before God in Revelations are thought to be archangels, though no one agrees on exactly which seven they are.

9.  Angels are intermediaries between the realms of heaven and earth. They are guardians of nations, states and cities as well as of individuals. The guardian angels of children are especially effective at protecting young ones because, according to Matthew 18:10, they always see the face of God.

## Know Your Archangels

The "magnificent seven" who stand before God, the archangels get more attention than any others in the heavenly host. Their names end in "el," meaning "brightness," "shining" or "radiant one" in various ancient languages. The best known archangels are:

*St. Raphael:* The name means "God heals" or "divine healer." In "The Book of Enoch," God tells Raphael to "heal the earth." He's noted for being especially friendly, kind and understanding to human beings. Raphael appears in human form to a young man in the Old Testament story of Tobit in Catholic Bibles. (See the Westminster Presbyterian entry for the story.) He may be pictured wearing sandals, carrying a traveler's staff and pouch, a container of healing balm, or loaves and fishes. Raphael is chief of the guardian angels and is especially concerned with travelers—those making both physical and spiritual journeys.

*St. Michael:* The meaning of his name is a question: "Who is like God?" First among all God's angels, Michael fought Lucifer and threw him into hell. He reportedly wiped out 185,000 Assyrian soldiers in one fell smote. Associated with courage and protection, Michael is known as the prince of light, God's champion, the viceroy of heaven, the leader of the archangels and the guardian of holy places. He is often pictured in armor with a shield and sword. When he's seen slaying a devilish serpent, he can easily be confused with St. George the dragon slayer.

In her book, "Messengers of Light," Terry Lynn Taylor offers an affirmation of St. Michael that's perfect for use on solitary walks or in dark parking garages. For protection in any situation, repeat the following three times: "Divine light of the highest order under the protection of the Archangel Michael."

*St. Gabriel:* A bringer of good news, a herald of transition, Gabriel is the angel of the Annunciation. He brings Mary the news of Christ's impending birth, a scene rendered by thousands upon thousands of artists throughout the centuries. He also tells Zechariah that his wife, Elizabeth, would bear the babe who grew up to become John the Baptist. He appears to the prophet Daniel twice: to interpret a vision, and to foretell the coming of the messiah. He is often pictured carrying a trumpet or horn, symbolizing the voice of God, or holding a lily, meaning purity. In Islamic tradition, Gabriel is the prophet Mohammed's guardian angel. His name means "strength of God."

The Archangels Raphael, Michael and Gabriel are all recognized as saints in the Catholic Church.

*Uriel:* With a name meaning "fire or light of God," Uriel presides over hell, meting out God's judgment. Some believe he is the angel who wrestled Jacob all night long, leaving his thigh out of joint. Another side of his nature is less brutish. He inspires writers and teachers and is known for his powers of transformation, prophecy and interpretation. He may be seen holding the keys to the gates of Hades, a sword, a scroll or a flame in the palm of his hand.

*"Learning to Fly,"* watercolor, Ann Engel.

# PART I: The Angel Tour

THE ANGEL IMAGES featured on the following pages are by no means the only ones in town. This listing is far from comprehensive. In fact, I'm certain there are dozens, if not hundreds, of angels that eluded me. (Angels are like that.) Neither is this a collection of only the best angel representations, though many mentioned here would be hard to top.

The angels in this book are the ones that came to me when I called. I placed ads in newspapers and magazines, surveyed people at angel seminars and classes, called upon friends and strangers, experts and angel aficionados. Most of the images I discovered in my search are included here.

They are contemporary and ancient. They are made of stained glass, wood, stone, brass, gold, steel and bronze. Some are tiny, others towering. The images are as varied as the ideas we hold about angels. Yet each of these images is an expression of faith. (Well, maybe not the Flying Dutchman at the Hennepin History Museum.) But in the main, these angels bear witness to belief in the divine, the unseen. As such, they are all heavenly.

Angels are especially present in churches. Visit enough and you'll begin to feel their presence.

In scouting angels, you'll find yourself in some of the most beautiful buildings in the Twin Cities. It's my hope that this book will encourage people to become tourists in their own home towns, exploring local churches and chapels the way travelers flock to cathedrals abroad. While we have no Gothic cathedrals here, we do have our own architectural treasures, full of beauty, local history and angels.

Looking for angels gives you an excuse to visit churches and other buildings you may not have seen before. It can also give you a new perspective on familiar surroundings. I've found many people overlook the angels that surround them every Sunday. One church member solemnly assured me there were no angels where she worshipped, yet the windows at her church are filled with them.

## Looking at Churches

Though I once worked for an architectural firm and have visited dozens of European cathedrals, I never did get those architectural terms nailed down. When I began my angel search, I vowed not to use architectural terminology to describe building spaces because most people aren't familiar with it. However, it soon became clear that avoiding these terms makes for some cumbersome prose.

Following are some of the terms used in this book:

ALTAR:     A communion table or the place that serves as the focal point or center of worship.

AISLE:     A passageway running parallel to the nave, often separated from it by columns. There may be one or two aisles on either side of the nave.

APSE:    A semicircular area that projects from a church or other building, located behind the altar.

CLERESTORY:    An outside wall that rises above an adjoining roof and contains windows. Clerestory windows line the nave above the aisle windows.

NAVE:    The main part of a church interior, especially the long central hall that rises higher than the aisles on either side.

NARTHEX:    A vestibule outside of the main body of the church, often just inside the main entrance.

PEDIMENT:    A triangular area forming the gable at the top of a building.

PENDENTIVES:    Triangular areas between arches.

PIER:    A vertical, structural support. A pier may support the end of an arch.

SACRISTY:    The area in a church where sacred objects and vestments are kept.

SANCTUARY:    The altar and the area surrounding it compose the sanctuary in a cross-shaped church. It is the most sacred part of the building. In other church designs, the sanctuary refers to the entire room where services are held. "Sanctuary" is used both ways in this book.

TRACERY:    Decorative openwork at the top of a stained glass window.

TRANSEPT:   In a cross-shaped church, the transept crosses the nave at a right angle. Also called the crossing, the transept forms the shorter part of the cross. The term also refers to the projecting ends of the transept that often hold windows.

## Do's and Don'ts

Not surprisingly, most of the angels in this collection are located in churches. Most churches welcome visitors. However, viewing works of art in a place of worship is a bit different from visiting a museum. Before you embark on your own angel adventure, consider the following do's and don'ts.

*Do call first* for times of services and other hours the church may be open. Some churches are open only for services; others are open certain hours during the day. Call to check the policy at the church you want to visit. If the church is open, ask which door to use. Sometimes main doors stay locked while an inconspicuous side door remains unlatched, admitting those in the know.

*Do ask directions* if you're unfamiliar with the neighborhood. Bringing along a good city map is a good idea, too.

*Do ask about group tours*. Many larger churches offer them. Even a group of friends may qualify for a guided tour. Be sure to mention that you are interested in seeing the angels so the guide can tailor the presentation appropriately.

*Do visit on a bright day*. That's when stained glass is at its best. Viewing dimly lit buildings is easier on sunny days, too. Remember, most churches are designed to look their best in morning light.

*Do bring binoculars or opera glasses* if you want to see all the details in a large church or cathedral, but please be discreet. Never use them during a church service.

*Do express your appreciation.* Tell church and staff members that you admire their building. They'll be flattered. Leave a few dollars in the offering box. They'll be grateful.

*Do be respectful.* A church is a place of worship. Visitors should keep their voices down and generally behave with decorum, if not reverence.

*Don't interrupt or disturb* a group or individual in prayer. Have you ever tried to pray or meditate while someone was snapping pictures behind you? It's not pleasant.

*Don't walk up onto the altar area,* into the sacristy or other areas not meant for the public. In some churches, alarms will sound.

*Don't touch the works of art*—stained glass and stone sculpture included.

*Don't disrupt a church service.* Talking, taking pictures, walking about, using binoculars and pointing are all disruptive. It's perfectly all right to glance about discreetly during the service, but save the walking tour until after the final blessing.

Be quiet, behave, don't touch, don't wander off. Can you tell I'm a mother? Now that we've had this little talk, let's be on our way.

*"Angel with Halo," watercolor, Ann Engel.*

# The Angels of St. Paul

*"Justice" mosaic, Cathedral of St. Paul.*

## CATHEDRAL OF ST. PAUL
239 Selby Ave., St. Paul
228-1766

In stained glass and stone, bronze and gold, angels are everywhere at the Cathedral, a St. Paul landmark designed by Emmanuel Masqueray and built between 1906 and 1915. In his book, "The Cathedral of Saint Paul: An Architectural Biography," Eric C. Hansen points out that ". . . like its ancestors in medieval Europe, (the Cathedral) is not only a house of worship, but a great theology book in stone." Its embellishments serve an educational as well as a decorative purpose. Many of the lessons the building teaches are about angels.

Before entering, gaze up at the graceful angel atop the sacristy, just west of the main dome. Her robes bounce in the breeze as she stands on tiptoe, head bowed in prayer, reverently gazing toward the Cathedral's sanctuary. This joyful sculpture by Ernest Pellegrini of New York has long been a personal favorite. It's also one of the most well-recognized angels in town. Below her, you'll notice two carved cherubs flanking a stone plaque above the sacristy's entrance.

For a stained glass lesson in angel lore, go in the Cathedral's Selby Avenue entrance and look up at the 24 windows in the spectacular dome. Designed by Chester Weston in the 1950s, the eight sets of three windows illustrate the celestial hierarchy—the gradations of angels. Angels, Archangels, Virtues, Powers, Principalities, Dominations and Thrones get three windows each. The Cherubim and Seraphim share the final trio of dome windows. Each grouping is identified with signs supported by graceful plaster angels. Like the heavenly beings they represent, these windows are positioned a little higher than humans, but not as high as God.

Seventy feet above the ground, four spectacular angels grace the pendentives, the triangular areas near the base of the dome, between the supporting arches. Designed by Michelangelo Bedini and executed by the Vatican Studios, each of these powerful, 25-foot-high figures stands on a cotton ball of a cloud against a sky of Venetian gold. They're composed of thousands of brightly colored tiles.

These angels represent the cardinal virtues: Prudence, Justice, Fortitude and Temperance. The upper corners of each virtue's realm are filled with cherubs carrying wreaths and torches.

The elaborate bronze canopy above the sanctuary is topped by two angels placing wreaths on the bronze clouds. With their dark patina, these figures are often difficult to see. (For best viewing, visit the Cathedral on a bright day. Better yet, attend a mass on a sunny Sunday morning, when all the lights are on and sunlight streams through the dome windows.)

Just as seven angels stand before God (Revelations 8:2), seven stained glass archangels stand guard over the holiest place in the Cathedral, the sanctuary. In each window, an archangel stands on a rainbow and holds a medallion representing one of Catholicism's seven sacraments. Designed by Bostonian Charles J. Connick, one of the foremost stained glass artists of his day, these windows are an exquiste combination of beauty and meaning.

As you look toward the altar, the first window on the left represents the sacrament of Baptism. The Archangel Gabriel holds a medallion showing the baptism of the Ethiopian eunuch by St. Philip.

To Gabriel's right, the Archangel Michael, in his armor, shows St. John the Evangelist confirming a youth. The sacrament is Confirmation.

Next is the sacrament of Holy Orders. The Archangel Zadkiel holds his emblem, the sword, and a medallion featuring Christ commissioning the apostles.

Dedicated to the Eucharist (Holy Communion), the next window shows the Archangel Raphael carrying a staff, a gourd and a traveler's pouch. He shows us a view of the Last Supper.

To Raphael's right the Archangel Jophiel, with a flaming sword, displays a view of Adam and Eve being united in Matrimony by God.

The Archangel Uriel holds a medallion showing Christ forgiving a sinful woman. The sacrament is Penance.

At the far right, the Archangel Chamuel holds an urn and an illustration of the apostles performing the sacrament of Extreme Unction, now called Anointing of the Sick.

The seven winged figures painted in the recesses above the stained glass archangels symbolize the seven gifts of the Holy Spirit: knowledge, counsel, understanding, piety, wisdom, fear of the Lord, and fortitude.

Other angels hover about the front of the building. Cherub faces top the columns in the Chapel of St. Peter to the south (left) of the sanctuary, and angels grace the ceiling. In the Chapel of the Sacred Heart, on the opposite side, angels with hands crossed over their hearts guard and praise Christ. Golden cherubs and plaster angels decorate the arches supporting the dome.

A series of bronze grilles serves as a backdrop for the sanctuary. Each grille is composed of eight medallions picturing saints and angels. Singing angels enliven the bottom row of medallions and inspire the singers in the choir stalls, just in front of them. A view of the Annunciation (the Archangel Gabriel's appearance to Mary) is depicted in one of the bronze medallions. The grilles can be examined closely from the Shrines of the Nations, the semicircular area behind the sanctuary.

A stained glass window picturing St. Clare with an angel in flight above her is included in the Shrine of St. Anthony, the first shrine on the south side of the sanctuary. (The noted stained glass maker Bancel La Farge created the windows in the shrines.)

Cherubs support polished marble medallions above each saint in the Shrines of the Nations. More cherubs decorate the medallions on the altars of St. John the Baptist, St. Therese of Lisieux and St. Boniface.

Once you've completed the tour of the Shrines of the Nations, stroll toward the back of the Cathedral. On your way, note the small round window above the Chapel of the Blessed Virgin on the south wall. The Archangel Gabriel makes an appearance here in stained glass designed by Connick. Carrying a lily, the symbol of purity, he tells Mary that God has chosen her to bear the Christ child. Red-winged cherubim, roses and other symbols of Mary decorate the band encircling this Annunciation scene. Another Annunciation window can be viewed in the chapel itself.

Cherubs can be found on the arches surrounding the doors to the narthex. Walk outside and gaze up at the sculptures over the building's main entrance. Two angels representing faith (holding a cross) and science (carrying a torch) perch there. Actually allegorical figures rather than angels, this pair holds a plaque inscribed in Latin with the words of John 1:9, "He was the true light that enlightens every man that comes into this world."

Most of us don't see real angels, but many believe we observe signs of their work. So it is with one "invisible" angel at the Cathedral. Located near the piers supporting the dome, the sculptures of Matthew, Mark, Luke and John were designed by a man from Sandy Hook, Connecticut. His name? John Angel.

## ST. JOHN THE EVANGELIST EPISCOPAL CHURCH
Portland Avenue at Kent Street, St. Paul
228-1172

An exceptionally beautiful church, St. John the Evangelist is designed in the Gothic Perpendicular style, an architectural design that originated in England in the 14th century. When leaving the church, it's almost surprising to find oneself on the corner of Kent and Portland in St. Paul and not in the English countryside.

Walk in the door on the Kent Street side of the building and up the stairs. You'll find two stained glass windows of angels in the narthex. The Archangel Michael, leader of the archangels, carries a flaming sword, and a shield with the scales of justice on it. Next to him is the Archangel Raphael, whose name means "God heals." These angels, God's defender and the divine healer, honor those who served in World War II: "In memoriam, those who gave their lives; In thanksgiving, those who returned."

On the opposite side of the narthex, the Virgin Mary and the Archangel Gabriel are depicted in a stained glass Annunciation

*Archangel Michael window, St. John the Evangelist Episcopal.*

scene. His wings are a brightly colored mix of dark blue, green, yellow and red. All three angels wear diadems, or crowns, symbolizing divine authority.

To the left of the sanctuary stands a human-sized angel carved of white Carrara marble in Florence, Italy, around 1900. The seashell she carries is filled with water during baptisms. Her long hair, flowing robes and large wings appear very realistic. (Note the detail carved into the wings' feathers.)

Carved wooden angels, their hands held in prayer, stand on either side of the altar. Between them is an amazing representation of the Last Supper, carved in wood by a Swiss artisan.

Above the altar is the Te Deum window. It illustrates a hymn of praise used in worship called the "Te Deum" (meaning "To God"), which reads in part . . .

> . . . All creation worships you.
> To you all angels, all the powers of heaven,
> Cherubim and Seraphim, sing in endless praise:
> Holy, Holy, Holy, Lord, God of power and might,
> Heaven and earth are full of your glory.
> The glorious company of apostles praise you.
> The noble fellowship of prophets praise you.
> The white-robed army of martyrs praise you. . . .

Christ is at the center of the window surrounded by saints, angels, apostles, martyrs and prophets—all praising God. The angels are just above Christ.

*Archangel Raphael statue, Church of St. Luke.*

## CHURCH OF ST. LUKE
1079 Summit Ave., St. Paul
227-7669

St. Luke's boasts some of the area's most extraordinary exterior angel sculptures. Archangels stand on either side of the main entrance, guarding the bas relief image of Jesus between them. The Archangel Michael offers strength and protection with his sword and armor. The Archangel Raphael holds his traveler's staff and a fish. The strong and powerful Michael and the guiding, healing presence of Raphael suggest the need for firmness in one's faith as well as love and compassion for all.

Eight angelic faces appear in the stone medallions arching over the main entrance. They are interspersed with symbols of traditional Christian values and beliefs such as hope, (an anchor), beauty and resurrection (a peacock), and justice (the scales).

There are yet more angels on the facade. In a relief sculpture over the west door, one of the cherubim, sword in hand, ejects Adam and Eve from the Garden of Eden. Angels join with saints in adoration of Jesus over the main entrance. And the Archangel Gabriel appears to Mary in an Annunciation scene over the east entrance, representing the coming of Jesus who will save humans from the sin of Adam and Eve.

Now look up toward the very top of the facade. Beneath the cross that tops the pediment is a statue of St. Luke. Above him is a lamb flanked by two angels.

Walk north along Lexington Parkway and you'll find a statue of Gabriel projecting from the corner of the baptistry. He seems to be pointing the way to the church entrance and, one can surmise, to eternal life. Beneath him, carved in the Bedford stone exterior, are the words he spoke to Mary at the Annunciation:

"Of his kingdom there shall be no end" (Luke 1:33). Be sure to climb the winding stone stairway to the porch just outside the baptistry for a better look at Gabriel.

The three major angels on St. Luke's exterior, Michael and Raphael in front and Gabriel on the west, look particularly ethereal after a snowfall, with their shoulders and wings blanketed in white. Winter, spring and fall, their angelic presence has watched over generations of St. Luke's Elementary School children crossing these busy streets on their way to class.

Continue around the back of the building to view the faces of 14 cherubim above the windows of the sacristy, to the east of the apse.

Designed in the Romanesque style by architect John T. Comes, St. Luke's Church was completed in 1925. Inside the church on either side of the sanctuary, you'll find elegant angels holding lanterns. The lanterns' black ropes contrast sharply with the white marble angels.

Above Christ's outstretched arms on the crucifix, two marble angels in horizontal flight pray for him. Two brightly colored mosaic angels decorate the base supporting the cross. Their wings and robes are pastel tones of purple, blue, yellow, gold and green. Between these angels, a mosaic pelican feeds its young. The pelican symbol, which stands for charity and also for Jesus' sacrifice, is used throughout the church. According to legend, the pelican feeds its young in times of famine by sharing its own flesh and blood. (Ornithologists assure me only mythical pelicans are so charitable.)

Three exquisite marble angels on the pulpit hold the torch of knowledge, the ten commandments (symbolizing the law), and the lamp of wisdom. Four marble angels, heads bowed in prayer, support the four corners of the baptismal font, to the left of the altar.

Gaze up at the clerestory level near the transept. There, carved in stone, the angels of Love and Mercy watch over the congregation.

Gabriel, robed in green and looking rather feminine, appears in an Annunciation mural above the entrance to the Chapel of the Blessed Virgin, to the left of the sanctuary. A host of angels, on the left, and humanity, on the right, await Mary's decision.

On the chapel's altar, two marble cherubs hold a garland of roses. Gabriel appears again in the stained glass windows on the left wall. His scroll reads, "Hail Full of Grace." The pane below Mary includes a small angel, rendered in black outline, in the upper corner.

Turn and walk toward the back of the church, stopping to note the statue of St. Therese and the cherubs that hold a garland of roses at her feet.

The last stained glass window on the west side of the church features the destroying angel of Passover, armed with his sword, in the lower medallion.

Before leaving, note the lyrical relief sculpture of Christ's assumption into heaven over the middle doorway. He's flanked by two adoring angels that, though sculpted of stone, appear lighter than air.

In the lower church two carved wooden angel candlesticks top six-foot high columns on either side of the old, unused altar at the back of the church.


## ST. GEORGE GREEK ORTHODOX CHURCH
1111 Summit Ave., St. Paul
222-6220

The old and the new blend beautifully at St. George's, an architecturally modern church where Byzantine style paintings—including many angels—grace the dome, apse and sanctuary.

*"Pantocrator," dome mural, St. George Greek Orthodox Church.*

*"Theotokos," apse mural, St. George Greek Orthodox Church.*

40

Architects and church building committees who want to avoid the sterile look of contemporary church design should plan a visit to St. George's. They'll find religious embellishments that speak to a centuries-old tradition of faith looking very much at home in a contemporary design featuring clean lines and light, open space.

The New York iconographer, Yousis, created an icon of the "Pantocrator," ("The All-Ruling Christ"), in the dome. In this arresting image, Christ holds a Bible with his left hand and gives a blessing with his right. He is surrounded by eight angels on a gold leaf background.

Icon paintings date back to the earliest days of Christianity. Tradition holds that the first icon was created by the evangelist St. Luke, who painted an image of the "Theotokos," (the "Ever Virgin Mary").

Later iconographers maintained the style established by the earliest icon painters. Images of sacred persons or Biblical scenes, icons were typically created by monks who fasted and prayed for many days before beginning their work. That's why an icon is often called a meeting place between heaven and earth. The tradition continues today. Contemporary iconographers often prepare themselves spiritually before painting and maintain a reverent attitude while working.

In the apse, the Virgin and Christ Child sit on a throne flanked by two beautiful angels in tones of blue, orange and green on a background of gold leaf. The Greek inscription translates, "Maria the Theotokos, the one who is wider than heaven." It refers to the mystery of the Incarnation by which the infinite God, who is so limitless that the universe cannot contain him, was contained in the virgin's womb.

Archangels appear on the doors at either end of the Iconostasis, or altar screen. (The Iconostasis is symbolic of the veil that separated

*Dome mural, the Rev. Richard Fale, Church of St. Agnes.*

the Holy of Holies from the rest of the temple in Old Testament times.) On the right is the Archangel Gabriel, dressed in a white robe and holding a lily. On the left is the Archangel Michael, holding his fiery sword.

Atop the Iconostasis are smaller icon paintings. The Annunciation and Resurrection scenes on the left side of the altar both feature angels.

Don't miss St. George's Greek Festival, held each fall. Visitors are invited to tour the building and enjoy traditional Greek food, music and dancing. It's a wonderful event for the whole family.

## CHURCH OF ST. AGNES
548 Lafond Ave., St. Paul
293-1710

(NOTE: The Twin Cities Catholic Chorale and 20 or more instrumentalists from the Minnesota Orchestra perform each Sunday at the 10 a.m. Latin High Mass except during Advent, Lent and in the summer months. On those Sundays, the ancient Gregorian chant is sung.)

To keep restless children quietly occupied during mass, St. Agnes' pastor, Monsignor Richard J. Schuler, encourages them to count the angels in the church. "There are more than 100 of them," he says. Searching for angels in this lovely Baroque style church is as much a delight for adults as it is for children.

Many can be found in the joyous view of heaven—all blue skies and fluffy clouds—painted on the interior of the dome. In this happy scene, all the saints and angels rejoice as Christ crowns St. Agnes of Rome in heaven. Angels turn toward Christ with an open Bible, a wreath and an incense burner, while others bear flowers and play horns. Adding to the feeling of joy and light, the saints and angels wear pastel yellow, gold, blue, pink, mint green and purple. The Rev. Richard Fale, a priest from Wisconsin, painted the scene in the summer of 1988. He died shortly thereafter.

Magnificent stained glass angels, robed in white, watch over the congregation from the small, round windows on either side of the dome. Their wings are feathered in tones of deep blue, green and purple. Gold-winged cherubs support these lovely images. St. Agnes' stained glass windows were created by the F.J. Mayer Company of Munich in 1930.

The most spectacular stained glass angels at St. Agnes are tucked away in the choir loft. Wait until after the service is completed and the musicians have descended the narrow, curving stairway near the main entrance. Then make your way up to the choir loft. Ask politely of anyone there if you can view the windows.

The first one, on the east side of the pipe organ, features St. Cecilia, patron saint of musicians, playing her organ while three cherubs flutter above her. Glance up at the top of the massive pipe organ and you'll see angels holding candelabra on either side.

Now carefully make your way to the opposite side of the loft, taking care not to bump the timpani. There you'll find a breath-taking stained glass window of two angels dressed in robes of deep violet and blue, playing the lute and violin. One has white sleeves decked with gold stars. With St. Cecilia and these lovely angel musicians for inspiration, it is no wonder St. Agnes is well known for its beautiful music.

Before descending the staircase, take in the view of the church from the choir loft. Designed by George Ries, the building spread out before you has been serving St. Agnes parish since 1912. You'll see cherubs above each of the tall, stained glass windows lining the nave. Early visitors will notice that all St. Agnes' stained glass comes vibrantly to life in morning light.

Downstairs, in the second window from the back on the east wall, you'll find the risen Christ flanked by two angels with their wings unfurled. One of the angels looks down at Mary and the apostles below.

A beautiful Annunciation scene is depicted in stained glass on the west wall near the front of the church. Gabriel looks powerful and masculine, though his wings are difficult to make out. Mary, dressed in blue and white, kneels as Gabriel gives her God's message. Her traditional white lilies grow by her side.

St. Agnes' sanctuary is thick with angels. On the right (west) side of the altar, a stained glass window pictures Jesus praying in the garden of Gethsemane on the night of his arrest when an angel appears to strengthen him (Luke 22:43). Here, the angel is shown holding the cup. A sleepy disciple can be seen in the background.

Two angels kneel and pray at either side of the altar, which was made in Italy in 1930. Two others stand playing their horns atop the altarpiece, their unfurled wings pointing straight up. Cherubs perch on both sides of the cross that tops the altarpiece.

Cherubic faces with golden halos decorate the altar railing, six to a side, and the pulpit. Another sits atop the pulpit's canopy.

To the left of the sanctuary is an altar to Mary. Two angels stand on top of the columns flanking Mary's statue. One prays as the other holds her hands over her heart. Three cherubs gather near Mary's feet. A golden cherub face decorates the arch above the statue. Two others grace the pedestal on which a crucifix stands. An altar to Joseph on the opposite side of the sanctuary is similarly embellished with angels.

A painting of Mary and her infant son surrounded by angels hangs on the wall above Mary's statue. Three angels, two of them

*Angel monument, Calvary Cemetery.*

46

capable-looking older women, kneel and pray in front of the mother and child. Two angel musicians hover above them in diaphanous gowns of white and green.

Winged cherubs support each station of the cross and decorate the small columns on either side of these 14 scenes from the life of Christ.

How many angels did you count? More than 100 are mentioned here. For an exact count, visit St. Agnes yourself. Try to be there on a Sunday at 9:55 a.m. when the church bells ring. Their wonderfully throaty tones seem to reverberate through to one's very soul.

## CALVARY CEMETERY
753 Front Ave., St. Paul
(Energy Park Drive turns into Front Avenue as it heads east across Lexington Parkway. The cemetery is between Lexington and Dale on Front.)
488-8866

Calvary Cemetery is a lovely, peaceful spot in the middle of the city. It's also loaded with angels. Go in the east entrance, across the street from the cemetery office. Continue straight through the first intersection. On your right, between two old cedar trees is the Archangel Gabriel, with his horn, on the Hahn monument.

Now take a right, then the next left and follow the road until you come to an island. A large angel holding a bouquet of flowers stands atop the Schmidt/Bremer monument on your left. Continue down the road and you'll see the Geist monument on the right with another angel. The Pellegrene monument, with a kneeling angel and a flower-decked cross, is about 100 feet beyond the Geist angel, four graves in from the side of the road.

Drive to the intersection and turn left. There you'll see the Benz monument with a lovely angel statue behind its own green hedge. Stay on this road as it swings around to the northeast and you'll find a monument marked James, with an angel sculpture carrying flowers.

Calvary is worth a visit to scout for angels even in the winter. All except the Pellegrene monument are easy to see from the car.

## More Angels

There are many more churches filled with angels in the area to explore on your own. Some of them are listed below. Again, be sure to call first for directions, to find out when the churches might be open for viewing and when services are held.

### ST. PAUL'S CHURCH ON THE HILL
1524 Summit Ave., St. Paul
698-0371

St. Paul's has angels in the stained glass windows in the apse, carved wooden angels in the chapel to Mary and a brass angel on the wall near the main entrance.

### PILGRIM LUTHERAN CHURCH
1935 St. Clair Ave., St. Paul
699-6886

Angels have become part of a lovely Christmas tradition at Pilgrim Lutheran Church. Starting the first Sunday in Advent, a set of angel candle holders is placed on the end of two pews. More angels are added each Sunday until Christmas, when at least a dozen angels line the aisle, in celebration of Christ's birth. Made by an artist and church member in the 1970s, the angels are papier-mâché painted brown and highlighted with gold.

## AQUINAS CHAPEL, UNIVERSITY OF ST. THOMAS
Cleveland Avenue near Ashland Avenue, St. Paul
962-6560

This lovely chapel is alive with angels. It was designed by Emmanuel L. Masqueray, the architect of the Cathedral of St. Paul and the Basilica of Saint Mary. Over the nave windows, painted angels hold banners describing the events illustrated in stained glass below. These are: Creation, the Fall, Nativity, Wisdom, Revelation, the Passion, the Promise and Elevation. Take your time "reading" the beautiful stained glass windows, which were executed by the noted artist Chester Weston. Above the sanctuary is a mural painted by Carl Olson of four striking angels, robed in white and carrying symbols of the faith. The colorful rose window on the facade shows the Holy Trinity. Two angels dressed in purple with teal-colored wings hold chalices beneath the hands of the crucified Christ. Four seraphs, with six wings each, are part of the design, as are the cherubs encircling the entire scene.

## BETHESDA LUTHERAN HOSPITAL AND REHABILITATION CENTER
559 Capitol Blvd., St. Paul
232-2000

A Paul Granlund sculpture of the Bethesda angel, who "troubled the waters" and healed the sick in Jerusalem, stands outside the hospital's east entrance.

## ST. BERNARD'S CATHOLIC CHURCH
197 Geranium Ave. W., St. Paul
488-6733

Angels playing trumpets herald God in the mural on the triumphal arch over the sanctuary. In the north transept is a striking stained glass window of the Virgin and Christ child surrounded by eight adoring angels.

## MINNESOTA STATE CAPITOL
75 Constitution Ave., St. Paul
For information, call 296-3962.
To arrange group tours, call 296-2881.

A carved marble angel is positioned over the middle arch of the Capitol's front entrance, protecting those who enter. Allegorical figures in the form of angels populate the two murals in the senate chambers, both by artist Edwin H. Blashfield. "Minnesota Granary of the World" features graceful winged geniuses, or spirits, on either side of the personification of Minnesota. "Discoverers and Civilizers

Led to the Source of the Mississippi" includes the winged spirits of Discovery and Civilization.

## ST. ADALBERT'S CHURCH
265 Charles Ave., St. Paul
228-9002

Two angels holding incense burners stand on either side of the altarpiece, two more are featured in the apse mural. Cherubs support the stations of the cross and various statues.

## ADVENT LUTHERAN CHURCH
3000 N. Hamline Ave., Roseville
633-3232

A mosaic of the Archangel Michael, holding the scales and a horn stands behind the altar. It was created in tones of beige, red and blue in 1961 by Peter Dohmen.

*"Angel in the Wind,"* watercolor, Ann Engel.

# The Angels of Minneapolis

*Carved wooden angel, Basilica of Saint Mary.*

## BASILICA OF SAINT MARY
88 North 17th St., Minneapolis
333-1381; Group tours available.

The Basilica of Saint Mary was designed to take people away from things of the earth and bring them closer to God. Within this magnificent building, a host of angels helps transport visitors a little closer to heaven.

A National Historic Landmark, the Basilica of Saint Mary was designed in the Beaux-Arts style in 1906 by Emmanuel L. Masqueray, the same architect who designed the Cathedral of St. Paul and about a half dozen other churches in the Twin Cities. The Basilica of Saint Mary was designated America's first basilica by Pope Pius XI in 1926. (A basilica is a Catholic church that is given certain ceremonial privileges.) It's well worth arranging a docent-led group tour of the building. You'll see areas of the church that are otherwise inaccessible to the public.

Dedicated to Mary, Christ's mother and Queen of all the angels, the Basilica is filled with angels of all kinds. Three choirs of angels surround the Virgin in the church's rose windows. Angels holding emblems of the faith grace each of the clerestory windows lining the nave. Stained glass archangels guard the entrances to the building.

The most recent angelic addition to the Basilica is the Choir of Angels, a spectacular series of six wooden angel statues, installed in the apse in November 1992. Hand carved in Italy in 1912, each angel is five feet tall and robed in gold and silver leaf.

The plans for the angels were part of a high altar design by an early 18th century Roman Jesuit architect. The Sisters of St. Benedict found his design in an archive in Rome in the early 1900s. (The documents they found didn't indicate whether the design had ever been executed.) They commissioned the creation of the altarpiece from these plans for their Sacred Heart Chapel at St. Benedict's Convent in St. Joseph, Minnesota. For 67 years, these lovely angels held a wooden crown aloft over the altar. When the chapel was renovated in 1981, the angels were removed and packed away.

Jay Hunstiger happened to see the angels when he walked through the carpenter shop where they lay in storage. He never forgot them. After Hunstiger became the Basilica's minister of worship in 1985, he took steps to bring the angels to Minneapolis.

The sisters hesitated. They didn't want to let them go. Yet they feared their beautiful angels might be damaged if they sat in the carpenter's shop much longer. Other people wanted the angels, too, including someone who planned to install them in a bar. The sisters decided their angels would feel most at home in the Basilica.

The Sisters of St. Benedict were special guests at the dedication of the Choir of Angels, Feb. 21, 1993, where this prayer was recited:

> Almighty God, whose Son our Savior manifested Your glory
> in His flesh, and sanctified the outward and visible to be a

means to perceive realities unseen: Accept, we pray, this representation of Your mighty angels; and grant that as we look upon them, our hearts may be drawn to things which can be seen only by the eye of faith; through Jesus Christ our Lord. Amen.

The Choir of Angels joins a multitude of other angels in and around the sanctuary. Angel musicians play their instruments in the five stained glass windows in the apse. Embossed steel angels enliven the decorative wrought iron grille around the sanctuary which features scenes from Mary's life. The six-foot, 150-pound sanctuary lamp features four bronze angels linking hands to bear the weight of a beeswax candle. Cherubs play harps near the top of the organ's pipes, and grace the altar candlesticks, the tops of the columns surrounding the altar, and the tabernacle (the ornamental box on the altar where the consecrated elements of the Eucharist are stored).

The elaborate altarpiece was carved in Italy in 1924. A marble statue of Mary stands on the baldachin, or canopy, over the altar. Eight angels adore her, two on each of the baldachin's four sides. Cherubs perch below the cross.

The Basilica's stained glass windows are its crowning glory. In contrast to its Hennepin Avenue neighbor, the Cathedral Church of St. Mark, the Basilica's windows were all installed at the same time in the mid-1920s, and were designed by one artisan: Thomas Gaytee. The company he established in 1918, Gaytee Stained Glass, remains a leading local maker of stained glass windows today.

The windows are especially beautiful at sunset when the west windows ignite with brilliant reds, oranges and golds and the east windows become strongly blue and green. The colors change constantly throughout the day. As part of the restoration of the building, old storm windows have been removed from the Hennepin rose window and the 12 dome windows, revealing brilliant colors that dart about the church as the sun moves across the sky.

The remaining 50-plus windows await the removal of the old storms.

The Immaculate Conception is pictured in the rose window in the west transept; the Coronation of Our Blessed Lady by the Holy Trinity is seen in the rose window on the east side. The rose window on the facade features the Madonna and Child Enthroned. The main image in each of the rose windows is encircled by three rings of angels representing the Seraphim, Cherubim and Thrones, the three orders of angels closest to God.

Between the Immaculate Conception and the Coronation windows, the story of the Blessed Virgin is traced in 20 scenes depicted within the clerestory windows. Above each scene, two large, winged angels hold emblems of the faith related to the Biblical and traditional stories illustrated below. Above these two angels, a third holds a ribbon inscribed in Latin with an invocation from the Litany of Loretto, a prayer to the Virgin. Atop them all is a large circular window featuring an angel whose scroll carries a verse from the Magnificat in Latin. (It translates, "My soul proclaims the greatness of the Lord, my spirit rejoices in God my Savior for he has looked with favor on his lowly servant . . .")

Beginning on the left side as you face the altar, the clerestory windows picture the Marriage of Mary and Joseph and proceed down the left side through the death of Joseph. They continue on the other side of the nave with the Miracle at Cana through the Passion and Death of Jesus to the Dormition (the falling asleep) of Mary near the right side of the high altar. The figures in the aisle windows below are of prophets and saints whose lives foreshadow or illustrate the scenes in the clerestory windows.

Note that the first two windows, the Marriage of Mary and Joseph and the Annunciation are reversed. In the Bible, Mary and Joseph are betrothed but not yet married at the time of the

Annunciation, when Mary conceives Jesus by the power of the Holy Spirit. Early parishoners insisted that, in their windows, Mary would not be unwed and pregnant.

Stained glass archangels stand guard over the entrances to the building and at the crossing. Above the communion rail on the west side stands St. Michael, armed with his sword and shield. Opposite him, St. Raphael holds a trident and fish. The front entrances are presided over by Jophiel, with a flaming sword, and Uriel, holding the book of knowledge, at the southwest corner. St. Gabriel, holding a staff topped with an orb and cross, and Chamuel, with a staff and chalice, hold forth at the northwest corner.

Step outside the main entrance and look back at the facade. You'll see cherubs above the portico's pillars. Far above, in the pediment over the rose window, four angels support the Virgin in a marble depiction of her Assumption into heaven.

Go back inside the church and walk up the west (left of altar) aisle past the sanctuary, and take a left at the shrine of St. John Vianney. You'll find yourself in the sacristy where there is a dramatic stained glass window of Christ the King flanked by two angels with red and gold wings.

The sacristy leads into the rectory, where you can ask the staff about The Friends of the Basilica, an interdenominational group dedicated to the preservation of this historic building. The Friends offer an angel needlepoint kit for sale. The design features a needle-point version of one of the Basilica's own cherubs. In addition, postcards, notecards, posters and other mementos are available in the church following each weekend service, and at the rectory Monday through Friday. Christmas cards featuring the Basilica's Choir of Angels are available during the holiday season.

*Angel window, Cathedral Church of St. Mark.*

60

## CATHEDRAL CHURCH OF ST. MARK
519 Oak Grove St., Minneapolis
870-7800; Group tours can be arranged.

Overlooking Loring Park since 1910, St. Mark's was designed in
the Gothic style by church member Edwin Hawley Hewitt, who
called this cathedral a place that "expresses . . . man's attitude
towards God." St. Mark's expresses the architect's personal attitudes
and style more than other churches he designed because church
leaders gave him the freedom to follow his muse in the creation
of this lovely cathedral.

The soaring arches, the dark carved wood, the light colored
stone, and the stained glass windows that flood the building with
light combine to give St. Mark's an appearance of great beauty
and grandeur without being heavy or ostentatious. The overall
feeling is warm, light and welcoming.

If you don't visit during a church service, go in the office entrance and let the receptionist know you'd like to visit the cathedral.
You'll be directed up the stairs to the cathedral's interior entrance.

Take a seat in front and close your eyes for a moment. Breathe
in the subtle, spicy aroma. A combination of incense, candle wax
and prayer, this is what a well-traveled friend refers to as "the
ancient smell." You'll find it in older churches and cathedrals
throughout the world.

Now, open your eyes and let them roam about the high altar
and sanctuary. The details of the ornate wooden carvings and the
well-populated stained glass window cannot be taken in at a single
glance.

The Ascension window, above the altar, features Christ surrounded by cherubs and angels, apostles, saints, martyrs and other
important figures of the church. Cherubs hold a scroll above Christ

and red winged angels playing instruments appear in the tracery pieces atop the entire scene. It was designed by noted craftsman William Bladden.

Fluffy white clouds drifted across a sunny blue sky the day I visited St. Mark's—a perfect day for viewing stained glass. The Ascension window put on a spectacular show as the sun darted in and out of the clouds. First the skin tones appeared most prominent. Then the purple and violet robes shone like jewels. Next the reds glowed and flamed. The windows change constantly with the light.

In the choir, the area between the crossing and the high altar, the carved stone capitals on the columns include a group of angel musicians playing various instruments and two angels holding a banner announcing that Christ has risen.

An Annunciation scene is depicted in one of the stained glass windows in the Hewitt Chapel, to the west of the choir. Just outside the chapel on the west wall, a green-winged angel is pictured in the Baptism of Jesus window, over the door.

Angels appear in the small circles above and between the larger medallions in all of the windows along the side aisles. All but three of the aisle windows were designed by the firm of Weston and Leighton. (Chester Weston, one of the partners of the firm, did a number of the windows at the Cathedral of St. Paul.)

The remaining aisle windows were designed by the renowned stained glass artist Charles J. Connick. Connick's are the second, fifth and sixth full length windows from the front of the church on the west side. He also designed the Te Deum window above the gallery and four clerestory windows: the two nearest the sanctuary on either side of the church.

Now turn and gaze up at the large clerestory windows on the east side of the building. You'll see a modern stained glass window filled with angels and scattered with stars. A banner at the bottom reads, "Glory to God in the Highest." Installed in 1986, it was designed by Dieter Spahn. Tones of blue, brown, rose, grey, yellow and white predominate. Composed of larger pieces of glass, this striking work is a lovely counterpoint to the older, more traditional windows in the building. Sunlight brings this scene brilliantly to life, making the stars dazzle like diamonds in the sky.

Angels appear in the tracery above the main images in the next two clerestory windows to the right.

Walk toward the back of the church to get a good look at the Te Deum window, opposite the Ascension window. This, too, is a Connick design. Here in stained glass, Christ on his throne is surrounded by angels, saints, prophets, martyrs and famous lay people of history, who all praise and adore him. The Archangels Michael and Gabriel appear in the tracery. Archangel Uriel can be found in the left center lancet, or opening, Raphael in the right center. Red-winged seraphim offer their praises on either side of Christ's throne. Look for King Edward VI of England wearing a gold crown in the lower corner.

In the aisle windows on the east side, we see the Archangel Gabriel appearing to Zechariah and angels appearing to the shepherds. Angels dressed in gold with pink wings offer praise at Christ's transfiguration. And an angel appears to Jesus in the garden.

Turning to the western clerestory windows, we see a relatively modern version of the children coming to Jesus, with angels overhead. To its left, angels appear over the image of Christ. The red-winged Archangel St. Michael, with shield and sword in hand, shows up here, too. The next window to the left features angels in the top of the design.

The Jaffray Chapel, within the Cathedral complex, has a stained

*"Abraham and the Three Angels,"* Pieter Pourbus, Hennepin Avenue United Methodist Church.

glass rendition of the artist Raphael's Sistine Madonna, 1513, with two cherubs looking up at Mary. In this familiar image, one cherub rests his head in his hand while the other props his chin upon folded arms.

## HENNEPIN AVENUE UNITED METHODIST CHURCH
511 Groveland at Lyndale Avenue, Minneapolis
871-5303; Group tours available.

At Hennepin Avenue United Methodist Church, angels appear in many of the sanctuary's exceptional stained glass windows, all designed by the famous stained glass maker Charles J. Connick. A few angelic faces are carved into the case work of the massive Sipe tracker pipe organ. A special treat for angel lovers is upstairs, in the church's own art gallery.

Park in the lot behind the church and ring the buzzer at the door where the church and the education wing join. As you enter, turn to your right, go through the glass doors and check in at the church office. Then go through the reception room, down the stairs and into the sanctuary.

Dedicated in 1916, the church was designed in the Gothic style by Minneapolis architect Edwin H. Hewitt, who also designed the neighboring Cathedral Church of St. Mark. The octagonal space with seating for about 1,000 is influenced by Ely Cathedral in England.

The stained glass windows in the piers, the vertical supporting structures, depict the four main events in Christ's life: the Nativity, Crucifixion, Resurrection and Ascension. Angels appear throughout.

Red-winged seraphim float above the Nativity scene illustrated in the northwest pier window. Above, more seraphim occupy three of the trefoils in the tracery, the ornamental stonework at the top of the windows.

Seven cherubim, symbolizing divine love and courage, surround Christ on the cross in the northeast pier window. Sorrowing angels appear above Mary, in the left opening, and St. John on the right.

The southeast pier window is a glorious Resurrection scene. Seven cherubim, this time symbolizing the seven spiritual gifts, embellish the flaming scarlet light surrounding Christ. Red-winged seraphim appear on either side and beneath him. The scene is witnessed by Mary, Mary Magdalene and the disciples John and Peter. Cherubim are seen in the tracery above.

The southwest pier window features Christ's Ascension into heaven. Musical angels and a chorus of cherubim are seen on either side of Jesus. Cherubim are also seen in the lower right and left tracery pieces.

The three windows located behind the balconies were designed to be viewed both from a distance and up close. Be sure to climb to the balconies to discover the delightful images hidden in the details.

The east transept window honors the four great Old Testament prophets, Isaiah, Jeremiah, Ezekiel and Daniel. Above each prophet is an angel; below, a scene from his life.

On the left is the prophet Isaiah. The angel above him holds a trumpet, a symbol of the evangelical prophet. In the medallion below, an angel touches the prophet's lips with a coal of heavenly fire (Isaiah 6:6). A weeping angel is pictured above Jeremiah, the sorrowful prophet. The angel above Daniel, the princely prophet, holds a crown. The praying angel above Ezekiel symbolizes the priestly prophet. In the upper shield of the tracery, the Archangel Michael, with his flaming sword, holds the symbol of Judah, the Lion.

The west transept window features the four evangelists, Matthew, Mark, Luke and John. In the tracery above them, the Archangel Gabriel, the herald of the New Testament, holds the symbol of St. Peter, the gold and silver keys.

The north window is devoted to the women of the Bible. On the left is Ruth of Moab, holding a sheaf of barley. Above her, an angel bears a shield with barley sheaves on it. Queen Esther holds a sprig of myrtle (her Hebrew name) which also appears on the shield of the angel above her. The angel above the Virgin Mary displays her symbol, the rose. The Archangel Gabriel appears in an Annunciation scene in the medallion below Mary. A spinning wheel, suggesting charity in clothing the needy, is on the shield of Dorcas of Joppa's angel.

St. Peter appears on the far left. Above him, an angel holds a shield inscribed with the cock, one of his symbols. On the extreme right is St. Paul. The symbol on the angel's shield is the three fountains.

Step outside the sanctuary and follow the signs to the art gallery on the second floor. There you'll find the T.B. Walker Collection of Religious Paintings in an art gallery designed specifically for the collection. An active member of the church, Thomas Barlow Walker (1840–1928) donated the land on which it was built. (The T.B. Walker Foundation also funded the art gallery that evolved into Walker Art Center.) Walker bought about 5,000 works of art worth an estimated $5 million over 52 years. Of his vast collection of paintings, only the small group at Hennepin Church remains intact.

The jewel of the collection is "Abraham and the Three Angels" by the Flemish painter, Pieter Pourbus, (1523–1584). Long thought to be the work of a lesser artist, the painting was reattributed in 1990 by George Keyes, curator of paintings at The Minneapolis

Institute of Arts. He called it a work any museum would be proud to own.

The painting shows Abraham entertaining three winged messengers of God who tell him that his aging wife Sarah will bear a son, Isaac (Genesis 18:1–12). Sarah laughs at the idea of becoming a mother at her age. The smaller scene on the right shows Abraham kneeling as he greets his heavenly guests. Among the many birds and animals in the scene is a turkey, from the "New World." This image helped date the work at 1565–1575, by which time trade with North America had become established enough for American turkeys to roam European farm yards.

On the west wall are three paintings from an altarpiece dedicated to the Virgin Mary by the Spanish artist Juan Correa de Vivar, (active 1549–1561). The artist painted in the late Gothic style, a bridge between Medieval and Renaissance works.

Elements of both Medieval and Renaissance styles are evident in "Joachim and Anna Meeting at the Golden Gate." Here the parents of the Virgin Mary meet in heaven. Correa doesn't have a command of perspective, so most of the painting appears rather flat, in keeping with the Medieval style of painting. Yet, a Renaissance style angel floats above the scene.

Legend has it that angels appeared separately to Anna and Joachim, announcing that Anna had conceived. Joachim was in the wilderness at the end of a 40-day fast when he received the news, while Anna was at home. This is known as the Immaculate Conception, which holds that Mary was conceived without sin and was therefore worthy to be the mother of God. (Many people mistakenly believe the Immaculate Conception refers to the conception of Jesus, not Mary.)

In "The Annunciation," the angel Gabriel and the Holy Spirit, shown as a dove, appear to Mary to announce that she will bear Jesus. The banner encircling Gabriel's staff reads in Latin, "Hail

Mary, full of grace, the Lord is with you. Blessed are you among women." A young, demure Mary is shown reading a book, a symbol of piety. Behind her are the white lilies of purity.

"The Nativity," the final of the three Correa pieces, shows two separate scenes. In the background on the right, angels bring glad tidings of great joy to the shepherds in the fields. In the foreground, Mary and Joseph kneel by the manger as the shepherds adore the child.

The collection includes four other Nativity scenes, all of which include angels: "Adoration of the Shepherds," by a follower of Casper de Crayer, Flemish, 17th century; "Adoration of the Shepherds," by a follower of Luca Giordano, Italian, 18th century; "Nativity with Adoration of the Shepherds and Magi," painted by an unknown Northern Italian artist in the mid-16th century; and "Holy Night," by an unknown 17th century artist of the Netherlands.

All five paintings include many traditional Nativity symbols. The stable, in ruins, signifies the disintegration of the pagan world with the coming of the Savior. The ox and ass, the lowliest of beasts, show that even the least among us can share in the wonder of Christ's birth. A column, broken off near the base, alludes to Jesus' life, cut short. A lamb, sometimes with its feet bound, symbolizes Christ, the sacrificial lamb, who gave his life to save ours. The angels stand for divine love and joy at the blessed event.

"The Assumption of the Virgin," by an unknown 17th century Italian artist, depicts the Catholic belief that the Virgin's body was taken up into heaven after her death and burial. The painting shows Mary sitting on a cloud while cherubim impel her upward. Look closely at the painting from different angles and you'll see angelic faces within the clouds surrounding Mary. Designed to be viewed from below, the painting was part of a screen behind an altar.

*Detail, chapel dome, Lakewood Cemetery.*

## LAKEWOOD CEMETERY
Hennepin Avenue at 36th Street, Minneapolis
822-2171

(NOTE: Lakewood's chapel is open to visitors Monday through Saturday, 8 a.m. to 4:30 p.m. except during memorial services. Call the cemetery the morning of the day you'd like to visit to get the day's schedule of services and plan your visit around them. Group tours may be arranged by calling the office.)

If you can only visit one place in search of angels, visit Lakewood. The Cemetery's exquiste Byzantine Chapel, completed in 1910, houses perhaps the most spectacular angels in the Twin Cities. A mosaic of twelve awe-inspiring angels, on a background of deep blue-green, is set in the dome of this jewel-like building. Their wings and the folds of their garments are outlined in gold and silver leaf. The wings of each angel are unfurled, offering protection; their feet are not shown, suggesting flight.

The four angels holding red roses are positioned at each of the major compass points, in reference to Revelations 7:1: "I saw four angels standing on the four corners of the earth."

The angels wear gowns of red, for life, a shade of yellow called pale, representing death, and blue, for resurrection. Though the three color schemes are repeated four times, no two angels are exactly alike.

The 12 angels relate to the 12 sons of Jacob, the 12 tribes of Israel, the 12 gates to the Holy City and the 12 apostles. They also suggest the 12 hours of a clock face and the 12 months of the year, for time and eternity come together under this sparkling dome. Designed so it can be used as a sun dial, the building can give you the time on bright days when sunlight pours through the 24 dome windows representing the hours of the day.

In the pendentives, four mosaic figures represent Faith (with purple robe), Hope (golden), Love (rose) and Memory (green). Above them, an inscription from the Song of Solomon reads: "Until the Day Break and the Shadows Flee Away." The inscription reminds us that fear and doubt depart along with the darkness at the first touch of morning light. The reference to the transforming power of light speaks to the angelic as well. For it is the angels, these messengers of light, who help us make the transition from this life to the next.

Six Italian artists, who had just completed work at the Vatican, set the 10 million, thumbnail-sized, mosaic tiles in the chapel's interior. The tiles themselves were made in Venice, placed on gummed cloth and shipped off to Minneapolis.

Local architect Harry W. Jones designed the exterior of the chapel in the Byzantine Romanesque style of the fifth century Haghia Sophia in Istanbul. Charles R. Lamb, of New York, designed the interior after Venice's San Marco Cathedral. The chapel's interior is said to be the most perfect example of Byzantine mosaic art in the United States.

Exiting the chapel, walk across the street and down the steps to the reflecting pool that leads to the Lakewood Memorial Mausoleum. Completed in 1967, the building includes 24 stained glass windows and mosaics designed by Willet Stained Glass Studios of Philadelphia.

Brilliantly colored angel musicians dance across the central windows on the second level, overlooking the reflecting pool. Mosaic angels decorate the areas between the windows. Other stained glass angels, including the angels of Jacob's dream, can be found in alcoves on the second level.

Established in 1871, Lakewood Cemetery covers 250 acres of gently rolling hills between Lake Calhoun and Lake Harriet. Local luminaries including Hubert H. Humphrey, T.B. Walker, Floyd B. Olson and Charles M. Loring are interred here.

Among the thousands of graves, I only found three angel monuments. Overlooking Lake Calhoun, a marble angel stands encased in glass beneath a set of Gothic arches on the Blake monument in section 3. (Maps are available in the office.) Inspiring carved angels carrying flowers top both the West and Heinrich monuments in section 42, on the south side of the cemetery.

## THE MINNEAPOLIS INSTITUTE OF ARTS
2400 Third Ave. S., Minneapolis
870-3131

In researching this book, I asked hundreds of people to tell me their favorite local angel image. A surprising number named Ernst Barlach's bronze sculpture, "The Fighter of the Spirit," which stands outside the Third Avenue entrance to The Minneapolis Institute of Arts. Commissioned by a church in Kiel, Germany, in the late 1920s as a memorial to those who died in World War I, the sculpture has an intriguing history that gives it layers of meaning.

In 1938, the Nazis removed the sculpture from the grounds of the University Church of Kiel. The work was cut into pieces, which were to be melted down. In what sounds suspiciously like angelic intervention, the pieces were spirited away by an anonymous art lover and hidden throughout World War II. After the war, the city of Kiel had the sculpture repaired and installed in a new location. A mold was made of the original during repairs and, in 1959, the Art Institute purchased what is believed to be one of the bronze castings from the original.

Some see an angel in "The Fighter of the Spirit." Some say the

*"The Fighter of the Spirit," Ernst Barlach, 20th century, The Minneapolis Institute of Arts.*

*"Winged Genius," ninth century* B.C., *The Minneapolis Institute of Arts.*

winged figure represents the spirit of a city that survived against the odds. Others see the spirit of truth and beauty that would not be silenced. Its powerful lines suggest strength, endurance and transcendence—angelic qualities all. Angel or not, Barlach's sculpture is a potent image that is now a landmark for art and angel lovers throughout the area.

We'll take a roughly chronological look at the angels inside the Art Institute. Many of the works mentioned here aren't true angels, but we'll stretch our definition to cover just about anything with wings.

### "WINGED GENIUS," NINTH CENTURY B.C.

To call this low-relief stone sculpture an angel may seem quite a stretch, indeed. Yet this towering work of art, housed in the second floor ancient art gallery, speaks to the very roots of angelic imagery. Among the earliest examples of the "angel" form, the Genius offers elegant evidence that winged, protective spirits have fascinated people for centuries.

In ancient Mesopotamia (then called Assyria), the winged genius, or spirit, guarded the monarch's palace and performed certain rites associated with a sacred tree. Sophy Burnham's "A Book of Angels" includes an illustration of a winged being from New York's Metropolitan Museum of Art that originally protected the same palace as the Art Institute's Winged Genius, (the palace of Ashurnasirpal II at Nimrud). She notes that the concept of the cherubim is "Assyrian in origin, where *karibu* means 'one who prays' or 'one who communicates.'"

### "TRIPTYCH," 1535–1538, PIERRE REYNAUD

Angels take on quite a different look in the Medieval gallery on the third floor of the museum. Cherubs hold back the green drapery surrounding the Virgin and Child in this enamel on copper triptych, a devotional object with three panels. Golden stars are strewn across the blue enamel sky.

## "IVORY DIPTYCH," ABOUT 1375
Intricately carved angels help tell the story of Christ's life in this French piece. Gabriel greets Mary in the lower left-hand corner and angels appear in the adjacent Nativity scene. Adoring angels flank the risen Christ in the middle row of carvings. This delicate work of art was used for private devotions.

## "MADONNA AND CHILD WITH SAINTS," 1339, BERNARDO DADDI
The Archangel Gabriel, in pink and gold, appears in the left pinnacle of this Italian triptych to proclaim Jesus' impending birth to Mary, sitting opposite him. Mary's expression spans the centuries, her gesture clearly saying, "Who, me?" Cherubs appear in the center panel of this three-part wooden altarpiece used for devotions in the home.

## "MADONNA & CHILD ENTHRONED," 1490, NICOLA DI MAESTRO ANTONIO D'ANCONA
Putti (Italian for cherubs) with pink and green wings peek down at Mary and Jesus from behind the golden draperies.

## "THE NATIVITY," WORKSHOP OF FRA ANGELICO, 1387–1455
Fra Angelico is well known to angel lovers for his depictions of angels, many of which are frescoes. In this Nativity scene, attributed to Fra Angelico's Florentine workshop, blue angels atop a stable adore the baby Jesus.

*"The Annunciation,"* Girolamo de Santacroce, *16th century, The Minneapolis Institute of Arts.*

"THE ANNUNCIATION," GIROLAMO DA SANTACROCE, 1503–1556
God and his angels keep close watch over the events unfolding
below in this delightful Italian version of the Annunciation. The
artist takes pains to make certain viewers understand that Mary
becomes pregnant by the power of the Holy Spirit at the Annunciation. He paints a baby hurtling through space between the Holy
Spirit, in the form of a dove, and the unsuspecting Virgin. An
animated Gabriel, robed in blue and looking very masculine,
delivers his message to Mary.

"THE CORONATION OF THE VIRGIN," 1408, MARIOTTO DI NARDO
The Florentine artist's exquisite painting, truly one of the museum's
great treasures, includes five angel musicians at Mary's feet.

"THE ELEVATION OF THE MAGDALEN," 16TH CENTURY,
PETER STRUB THE YOUNGER
This curious German work illustrates the legend of Mary Magdalen.
Angels and cherubs propel the saint heavenward. Tradition holds
that, after the Crucifixion, Mary Magdalen went to Marseilles,
France, where she worked fervently for the early church, con-
verting thousands to the faith. Then she went to live in seclusion.
During this period of isolation, angels visited her seven times a
day, lifting her up to catch a glimpse of heaven.

"PIETÀ AND PANELS OF ST. JOHN AND ST. CATHERINE," LATE 15TH
CENTURY, BY THE MASTER OF THE ST. LUCY LEGEND
You won't see any angels on the front of this triptych. Take a
peek at the backs of the two outer panels and you'll discover an
Annunciation scene, with Gabriel on one side and Mary on the
other, designed to be viewed when the triptych is closed.

"Angels with Attributes of the Passion," 1612–1627,
Simon Vouet
A somber pair of angels are the central figures in these two paintings by the French artist Vouet. One canvas depicts a female angel
holding a silver pitcher (itself decorated with a cherub), a tray and
a cloth, in reference to Pilate, who washed his hands of responsibility for Christ's Crucifixion. The companion painting shows
a male angel carrying the inscription from the cross which reads,
"Jesus of Nazareth, King of the Jews," in Hebrew, Greek and Latin.

"The Union of England and Scotland," 1630,
Peter Paul Rubens
The great Flemish painter, famous for his highly dramatic Baroque
scenes, here illustrates the union that ended rivalries between
England and Scotland. Two fleshy cherubs fly overhead with the
coat of arms of the newly formed United Kingdom while a third
ignites a pile of weapons, which will no longer be needed due
to the new union. Meanwhile, personifications of England and
Scotland crown Charles I King of Scotland.

"The Annunciation," Dutch, 17th century, Dujardin
A blond Gabriel blows in on a cloud, his blue robes billowing
behind him, and surprises Mary, who is dressed in the same colors
as the angel.

Various works, 17th–19th centuries
The angel image was rarely used by Christian artists until the early
fourth century because of fear of association with the winged gods
of Greek and Roman mythology. The Art Institute has many
works featuring winged creatures of mythology, including "Venus
and Adonis," by Nicolas Mignard; "The Union of Love and

Friendship," by Pierre-Paul Prud'hod; the bronze sculptures "Boreas Carrying Off Orithyia" and Francois Rude's "Hebe and the Eagle of Jupiter;" and Alfred Gilbert's marble sculpture, "The Kiss of Victory." While they do not illustrate angels, these works are nonetheless compelling to those fascinated by winged beings.

### "IMMACULATE CONCEPTION WITH STS. FRANCIS AND ANTHONY OF PADUA," 17TH CENTURY, GIOVANNI BENEDETTO CASTIGLIONE

Continue through the paintings galleries and take the marble stairway to the second floor. Near the base of the stairs, you'll find Castiglione's massive Italian Baroque painting. Note the angels floating at Mary's feet.

That's the end of our angel tour of the Art Institute. There are more angels flitting about the museum—decorating urns and embellishing pieces of china—but those listed are my favorites.

## WESTMINSTER PRESBYTERIAN CHURCH
Nicollet Mall at 12th Street, Minneapolis
332-3421

A marvelous haven for angels right downtown, Westminster Presbyterian is a not-to-be-missed stop on any angel tour. Ring the bell at the office entrance on the 12th Street side of the building. (Tell the receptionist you'd like to look at the church and she'll buzz you in.)

Once inside, go up the stairs, turn left and walk down the long hallway. Just outside the chapel, two radiant stained glass angels welcome the faithful. Encased in glass and illuminated from behind, they are superb examples of stained glass artistry. Though they are

*Angel windows, attributed to Tiffany Studios, Westminster Presbyterian Church.*

not signed, local experts believe the windows were executed by Tiffany Studios or Tiffany-trained artisans. They offer one of the few opportunities in town to get face-to-face with a pair of four-foot angels.

Depicted in tones of soft yellow, white, beige and sand, these lovely creatures stand on a cliff above a purple and teal sea. One holds a Bible inscribed, "Be thou faithful unto death and I will give thee a crown of life." The other's Bible reads, "Faith is the substance of things hoped for, the evidence of things not seen." Originally installed over the south balcony of the sanctuary, these windows were restored in the late 1980s and placed here in memory of Thomas M. Crosby.

Just around the corner is Westminster's Gothic-style chapel, built in 1937. Angels appear at the tops of the stained glass windows lining the nave. The angels each hold a shield bearing a symbol of the faith including a ship, a globe, the Ten Commandments, a lamb, a cross, the Bible, a lily, a crown, a star and a dove. These windows were designed by Henry Lee Willet of Philadelphia.

The medallions below depict Biblical and religious scenes. An angel is pictured in the window closest to the front of the chapel on the right side. The stained glass at the front of the chapel shows angels adoring Christ at his Crucifixion and Resurrection.

Retrace your steps and enter the sanctuary. Now fix your gaze on the north rose window, overlooking 12th Street and prepare for a delightful surprise. As you read the stories in the finely detailed stained glass, you'll discover the entire window is dedicated to the angels. The central circle and the eight circles surrounding it all illustrate Biblical stories that move forward on the wings of the angels.

Given to the church in the 1920s, this beautiful stained glass angel study was designed by Charles J. Connick of Boston, who created all the windows at Hennepin Avenue United Methodist Church and some at the Cathedral of St. Paul, the Cathedral Church of St. Mark and several other local churches. Connick's windows gracefully combine words and images, light and shape and color.

The large, central circle features the Archangel Raphael and his young charge, Tobias, fish in hand, with the words of the 91st Psalm, "He shall give his angels charge over thee, to keep thee in all thy ways." Angels surround them on all sides. It's curious that Raphael and Tobias are featured so prominently in a Presbyterian church, since the Book of Tobit, which tells of their adventures, is included in only the Catholic version of the Bible.

As the story goes, the blind and elderly Tobit sent his son, Tobias, on a long journey to retrieve some money he had deposited with a relative years before. The man Tobias hired as a guide was actually the Archangel Raphael, disguised in human form. Raphael proved to be an exceptional guide for the young traveler. At camp the first night, when a huge fish leaped out of the river, Raphael told the boy to grab the fish, cut it open and keep its gall, liver and heart for future use. Indeed, these odd "medicines" did come in handy.

Once at their destination, Raphael encouraged Tobias to ask his host for the hand of his daughter, Sarah, in marriage. Tobias was hesitant, since Sarah had married seven times before and all her husbands had dropped dead on their respective wedding nights. However, Raphael told Tobias how to drive the husband-hating demon from the girl, using the fish liver and heart. Following the angel's instructions, Tobias survived his wedding night. Sarah's parents, overjoyed that their daughter finally had a live one, gave Tobias half of all their wealth.

When the bride and groom returned home, Raphael told Tobias to smear his father's eyes with the fish gall, which Tobias still carried. The old man's sight was miraculously restored. Later, Raphael revealed his true identity to Tobit and Tobias, told them to praise God always and then disappeared.

Perhaps Connick selected the story of Tobias and Raphael because he knew Minnesotans of all faiths enjoy a good fish story. More likely, he chose it because the tale expresses so many attributes of the angels: They often come to us in disguise to offer assistance, guidance, protection, wisdom, love and healing. They insist all thanks and praise are due only to God, whom they serve. Once their work is done, they return swiftly to the heavenly realm.

The outer circle of medallions illustrate other angelic apparitions in the Bible. In the 12 o'clock position, we see the holy family fleeing into Egypt to escape Herod's wrath, with an angel hurrying them along. The passage reads "(An) angel of the Lord appeared to Joseph" (Matthew 2:13).

Moving clockwise around the window, the next medallion reads "(An) angel of the Lord came to Peter." Peter is shown in chains as an angel comes to free him from his prison cell (Acts 12:7). This is just one of the instances in which angels spring disciples from jail.

"(An) angel of the Lord troubled the water" (John 5:4), refers to a healing pool in Jerusalem that drew many sick people. An angel would appear and stir up the water. The first person to enter the roiling pool was healed of all ailments. In the window, water springs from an angel's hand, while a man, woman and child await healing.

The next medallion shows a red-winged angel giving food to Elijah in the desert. The angel said, "Arise and eat," (I Kings 19:5) and the food and drink Elijah took fortified him for a journey of 40 days and 40 nights.

In the six o'clock position, we see an angel blessing a mother and child. The words "The angel of the Lord called to Hagar,"

(Genesis 21:17) refer to Sarah's maid, Hagar, who bore Abraham a son, Ishmael. After Sarah and Abraham's son Isaac was born, Abraham sent Hagar and Ishmael away. It was then that the angel appeared to comfort and reassure her.

The next medallion illustrates the testing of Abraham's obedience and faith. At God's request, Abraham tied up his beloved son, Isaac, and prepared to offer him as a sacrifice. As he was about to plunge a knife into the boy, an angel "called unto Abraham" (Genesis 22:11) to save the child.

In the nine o'clock position, angels attend to Jesus in the desert after he overcame the devil's temptation. The words of Matthew 4:11, "Angels came and ministered unto him," surround an image of Christ and two angels, one of whom enfolds Jesus in its wing.

In the final medallion, we return to the Nativity. An angel is pictured in the center, with a lamb below and shepherds on either side. "The angel of the Lord came upon them" (Luke 2:9) is inscribed within the familiar scene in which the angel proclaims the good news of Christ's birth.

Angels play minor roles in other sanctuary windows. One illustrating the 23rd Psalm is found just west of the angel window. On the lower left, angels lead the pilgrim beside still waters. An Annunciation scene is included in the southeastern window on the main level that is dedicated to Christ's childhood. Angels decorate the "Praise" window on the second level, to the east of the south rose window. They surround Christ in the central medallion of the south rose window. Angels bear the symbol of the Holy Spirit at the top of the next window and stand in prayerful respect of the martyrs and churchfolk pictured below. These windows were all designed by the Willet Studios of Philadelphia and installed during the 1950s and 1960s.

Westminster Presbyterian's congregation has been meeting in

the present church since 1897. The previous church, built in 1883, was located at Seventh Street and Nicollet Avenue, where Dayton's now stands. Westminster's first church building was located on Fourth Street between Hennepin and Nicollet avenues.


## FIRST CONGREGATIONAL CHURCH OF MINNESOTA
500 Eighth Ave. S.E., Minneapolis
331-3816

Built in 1888, and designed in the Richardson Romanesque style by Ohio architect Warren Hayes, First Congregational Church's sanctuary is home to two lovely stained glass angels.

The most dramatic window features an angel in flowing white robes that drape dramatically around her, as if blown by a heavenly breeze. She floats among the billowing clouds holding a scroll that reads "Blessed are the pure in heart for they shall see God." Her face is very painterly; her rosy cheeks framed by short blond curls. This beautiful window, designed by Tiffany Studios, is sometimes referred to as the black angel because it turns black at sunset.

A guardian angel window is installed next to the Tiffany window. This angel watches over a young boy who is about to chase a butterfly off the edge of a cliff.

These windows are unusual in that the images are raised up off the backgrounds, giving them a three-dimensional quality. Called "plating," this technique was often used by Tiffany and others to enhance certain window colors.

Before leaving, look up and to your left near the back of the church. On the north wall, you'll see another Tiffany window, this one depicting a river at sunset, its banks rich with trees and flowers.

*Angel with scroll, Tiffany Studios, First Congregational Church of Minnesota.*

*Angel baptismal font, T. Stein, Our Lady of Lourdes.*

## OUR LADY OF LOURDES
One Lourdes Place, Minneapolis
379-2259
Group tours may be arranged by calling 333-9016 or 339-1162.

Designated a U.S. historic landmark in 1934, Our Lady of Lourdes, the oldest continuously used church in Minneapolis, has played an important role in Minneapolis history from the earliest days to the present. Near this spot in 1680, Father Louis Hennepin first sighted and named the Falls of St. Anthony. More recently, the church served as the cornerstone for neighborhood redevelopment efforts. Coincidentally, an angel plays a role in the history of this unusual church.

In the vestibule, you'll find an enlarged photograph of the original limestone building, constructed from 1854 to 1857 by the First Universalist Society in a Greek temple style. Many of the New England free-thinkers who helped found Minneapolis belonged to this congregation. In keeping with their East Coast aesthetic, the New Englanders built a Yankee style meeting house with simple, unadorned lines.

Over the next 20 years, the population of the area changed. Many early residents moved out, and the neighborhood became home to a large French Canadian population. In 1877, the building was purchased by the Catholic French Canadian community which had been a part of the nearby St. Anthony of Padua parish, the first Catholic parish in Minneapolis.

The new owners transformed the building into a French Provincial church, a style typical of their native Quebec. A mansard style transept was added to the east end of the building, followed by a bell tower, sacristy and vestibule.

Today the building reflects the styles and cultures of both the

Yankees and the French Catholics, two important early influences in local history.

In 1971, the First Universalist Church presented Our Lady of Lourdes with a marble angel baptismal font in honor of the congregations' shared history.

The four-ton marble sculpture had been used by the Universalists for 80 years. The angel was carved by T. Stein in Copenhagen in 1891, and purchased by the Rev. James Harvey Tuttle, minister at First Universalist Church, as a gift to his congregation. It's the only known copy of Thorwaldsen's "Kneeling Angel," carved in Rome in 1827. Located on the east side of the sanctuary, the kneeling angel holds a seashell in its hands and wears a garland of flowers on its head.

Other angels make Our Lady of Lourdes their home. As you enter the church, you're greeted by two small angel statues above the holy water fonts. Plaster angel statues stand guard on either side of the tabernacle on the altar.

An important part of the early history of Minneapolis, Our Lady of Lourdes has been central to more recent local developments.

In 1968, the church was scheduled to be closed down and boarded up. Recognizing the significance of the building to redevelopment efforts, city officials persuaded the archbishop to keep the church open. The neighborhood changed again as St. Anthony Main and Riverplace developed around the church.

Meanwhile, Our Lady of Lourdes embarked on its own restoration effort, much of it financed by the sale of Tourtieres, traditional French meat pies made by parishioners. These delicious French specialties can be purchased frozen at the parish office. Proceeds are used to continue the restoration of this historic building.

## More Angels

### ST. BONIFACE CATHOLIC CHURCH
Second Avenue and Second Street N.E., Minneapolis
379-2761

Two praying angels guard the entrance to the church. Inside, four stone angels watch over the congregation from the base of the ceiling arches. Angels praise the Virgin Mary in a stained glass window on the north side of the church. A set of cherubs, each with two pairs of wings, is among the medallions decorating the arch over the sanctuary. On the altar, two small praying angels guard the tabernacle.

### STS. CYRIL AND METHODIUS CHURCH
1301 Second St. N.E., Minneapolis
379-9736

Graceful angels in pastel colors top each of the stained glass windows in this church, built in 1916. Cherubs gather at Mary's feet in a window on the south side of the building. Angels holding the bread and wine flank Christ in a painting in the apse.

### GETHSEMANE EPISCOPAL CHURCH
905 Fourth Ave. S., Minneapolis
332-5407

Gethsemane boasts three large angel stained glass windows. Turn to the left as you enter the main doors on the Fourth Avenue side of the building. There you'll find an Annunciation scene in stained glass. The Archangel Gabriel floats in on a cloud wearing white robes embroidered with gold patterns to make his announcement to the Virgin Mary. In the south transept, a red-robed angel blows an unusual horn. Above her, praying angels and angelic musicians praise Christ. Note the large glass "jewels" embedded in the window. To the left of the altar, a stained glass guardian angel keeps watch over her young charge. Below them are the words of the 91st Psalm: "He shall give his angels charge over thee."

## THE AMERICAN SWEDISH INSTITUTE
2600 Park Ave., Minneapolis
871-4907

Angels and cherubs are a recurring motif throughout this mansion, built by publisher Swan J. Turnblad between 1904 and 1907. More than 50 ornately carved cherubs are part of the decorative woodwork in the music room. No two cherubs are exactly alike. Butterflies and moths as well as birds may have inspired the distinctive wing designs. The music room angels and the finely detailed cherub on the dining room ceiling were carved by Swiss-born artisan Ulrich Steiner. After completing the cherubs, Steiner reportedly said he never wanted to carve another one as long as he lived. Also look for angels and cherubs in the decorative plaster ceilings, the imported porcelain tile stoves, and over the fireplace in the grand hall.

## HENNEPIN HISTORY MUSEUM
2303 Third Ave. S., Minneapolis
870-1329

The Archangel Gabriel, in the form of a weather vane, once flew atop the Winslow House Hotel, which was located near St. Anthony Falls. The angel weather vane now resides in one of the museum's first floor galleries. Presiding over the reference room is the Flying Dutchman, a folk art figure of a winged man holding an ear of corn like a torch in his outstretched hand. A promotional item for Minnesota Moline tractors, the Dutchman isn't exactly an angel, but he's just too wonderful to ignore.


## ST. STEPHEN'S EPISCOPAL CHURCH
4439 W. 50th St., Edina
920-0595

Four carved wooden angels kneel atop tall posts on either side of the altar. Their wings are spread and extend straight up as they kneel and hold candles. The stained glass window behind the altar includes an Annunciation scene, angels praising the risen Christ, the angel at the tomb on Easter morning and an angel coming to Christ in the garden. A few angels appear in the windows on the north side of the nave, including the angel that escorted Adam and Eve out of the Garden of Eden.

## CHURCH OF THE ANNUNCIATION
509 W. 54th St., Minneapolis
824-0787

A huge, modern Annunciation scene fills the windows on the north side of the church, opposite the altar. The stylized stained glass mural shows the Archangel Gabriel on the right, Mary and the Holy Spirit in the middle panel and another angel, upside down and carrying a sword, on the left. The sword-bearing angel is driving Adam and Eve from Paradise.

## ST. JOHN THE BAPTIST EPISCOPAL CHURCH
4201 Sheridan Ave. S., Minneapolis
922-0396

Installed in 1935, the Resurrection window above the altar shows the angel at the empty tomb on Easter morning. The other angel windows were installed in the early 1960s. The first window to the left of the altar shows the angel calling out to Abraham to stop him from slaying his son, Isaac. In the next window, an angel holds a burning coal to the lips of the prophet Isaiah. The Annunciation is featured in the next window.

## MINDEKIRKEN: THE NORWEGIAN LUTHERAN MEMORIAL CHURCH
Franklin Avenue and 10th Avenue S., Minneapolis
874-0716

A white-robed angel at Christ's tomb informs the women that "He is Risen," in this beautiful painting of the first Easter morning. The work is thought to be a copy of the Axel Ender painting in the church at Molde, Norway, though some say the painting at Kampen Church in Oslo is the original. Mindekirken's painting is installed in an ornate, wooden altarpiece and surrounded by carved wooden roses. The altarpiece was carved in the traditional Norwegian style by church member Leif Melgaard. Mindekirken has served Norwegian-Americans in the region since 1922, and continues to offer services in both English and Norwegian.

## MOUNT OLIVET LUTHERAN CHURCH
5025 Knox Ave. S., Minneapolis
926-7651

The Paul Granlund sculpture "Jacob and the Angel" stands on a pedestal just outside the administrative offices. Jacob and the angel are combined in one form. The angel feathers on Jacob's arms and legs suggest a flurry of limbs and wings as Jacob wrestles with the angel all night, not stopping until he receives his blessing (Genesis 32:24). A larger version of this sculpture is installed outside the north entrance to Vickner Hall at Gustavus Adolphus College in St. Peter, Minn.

(Writer and teacher Janet Hagberg keeps a photo of "Jacob and the Angel" taped to her computer as a reminder that her best writing efforts come when she wrestles with her angel as Jacob did. Hagberg refers to this sculpture in a class she teaches at The Loft called, "The Spirituality of the Writing Process." Call The Loft at 379-8999 for more information about the class.)

*Penance window with Archangel Uriel, Charles Connick, Cathedral of St. Paul.*

*Detail, chapel dome, Lakewood Cemetery.*

*Angel musicians window, Church of St. Agnes.*

*Angel monument, Calvary Cemetery.*

*Nativity window, St. John the Baptist Church, Vermillion.*

# Angels Out of Town

PLAN A LEISURELY drive in the country to check out some of the angel havens listed below. All are less than an hour's drive of the Twin Cities. Be sure to get a detailed map. Some of these towns are very small.

## ST. MARK'S CATHOLIC CHURCH
301 Fourth Ave. W., Shakopee
445-1229

It's worth a visit to St. Mark's just to see the dramatic carved wooden altarpiece. The church also boasts a guardian angel stained glass window that shows an angel carefully watching over two children, who are picking flowers on a steep hillside overlooking a lake. Other windows depict the Easter angel and the Virgin Mary surrounded by cherubic faces on an azure background.

## GUARDIAN ANGELS CHAPEL, ST. ELIZABETH ANN SEATON PARISH

Fourth Street and Ramsey Street, Hastings (Two blocks east of Hwy. 61)

437-4254

Stained glass windows of three archangels in a modern design by Gaytee Stained Glass grace the "gathering place" just inside the north entrance. Angels also appear on the doors.

## CHURCH OF ST. JOSEPH

23955 Nicolai Ave. (Hwy. 61), Miesville

437-3526

Angel holy water fonts greet you as you enter this lovely country church. Angels abound in the beautiful stained glass. Six angels float over the sanctuary in a striking apse mural. Cherubic faces appear in two of the lunettes in the apse. Brush up on your Latin before you visit and you'll be able to read the Beatitudes in the nave windows.

## ST. MARY'S CATHOLIC CHURCH

8433 239th St. E. (Hwy. 50.), New Trier

437-5520

Carved wooden angels playing trumpets stand atop the canopy over the altarpiece. Gabriel appears to Mary in a stained glass Annunciation scene on the east side of the nave.

## ST. JOHN THE BAPTIST CHURCH
106 Main St. W. (Co. Rd. 66), Vermillion
437-5652

More than three dozen angels abide at St. John's. The church is a testament to the faith of the farming community that built it in 1913. Angel musicians appear in a Nativity scene in the west transept window. In another window, an angel at the empty tomb announces Christ's Resurrection. Angels are featured in paintings over the triumphal arch and on the altarpiece. Two sacristy doors feature full length stained glass angels. They are unusual for they are pictured with tongues of flame above their heads, like those that descended upon the apostles when they received the Holy Spirit. Stained glass cherubs perch above the sanctuary doors. Cherubic faces grace the communion rail, along with grapes and shafts of wheat. Angels and cherubs decorate the side altars to Mary and Joseph.

*"David,"* *watercolor, Ann Engel.*

# PART II: Angelic Encounters

IN THE FOLLOWING pages, local people describe how their lives have been touched by the angels. All of these accounts are true. For the sake of privacy, some contributors asked to remain anonymous or to have only their first names published.

In his 1993 book, "Know Your Angels," John Ronner says some people might explain these types of experiences as "synchronicity," or meaningful coincidence. Others might say these encounters are the product of the subconscious mind, or even an active imagination. For me and for those whose stories appear here, however, the explanation is clearly the angels.

If you read enough books about angels, you'll find the same angelic experiences reprinted again and again. Not so with these stories; not one has ever been published before.

These stories differ from other collections of angelic experiences in another way. Not all of them are dramatic or spectacular tales of angelic intervention. That's because these spectacular appearances are just one of the ways angels make themselves known.

I find reading accounts of miraculous angel stories inspiring, but after closing the book I often think, "Well that's nice, but that kind of thing never happens to me." Just because angels don't appear to me regularly and haven't rescued me from a life or death crisis doesn't mean they aren't active in my life. There are many ways to experience the angels' love for us—some are just more flashy than others.

My own contributions to the following section are far from dramatic. They credit the angels for help in such unexciting matters as backing out of the garage safely. I include them to show that angels' help doesn't always come like a bolt out of the blue. In small, quiet ways, the power of God, expressed through the angels, can help us in the smallest details of daily life. These little stories show the process—or at least how it works for me and for others.

I hope all of these stories, the miraculous and the mundane, will help you recognize the angels' work in your own life and help you to live more in tune with the angels. When we ask them for assistance, recognize their help when it comes, and thank them for their blessings, we encourage the angels to become ever more active and helpful in our lives. And I can't help but believe that's just as God intended.

## How Angels Appear

Angels come to us in a variety of ways. Some people actually see angels in their full regalia—with wings, harps and halos. Sometimes angels come disguised in human form, as did the Archangel Raphael in the story of Tobit. An angel may also come as a bird or an animal, a quiet voice, a gentle nudge or a gut feeling. Some people may feel an invisible force, holding them back from danger. Others hear the angels singing. A family friend who prayed for my father every day of his long illness said she heard the angels sing for two weeks after he died.

Angels will come to us in a way that's best suited to each individual. If you've always thought of angels as winged beings in flowing robes, that may be how they would appear to you. If you think of angels as pure love, you may experience them as a warm, tingling feeling over your heart. A visually oriented person may see radiant colors. A verbally oriented person may hear spoken messages.

No single mode of perceiving angels is necessarily better than another. You don't have to see angels as other people do to have a valid angel experience. If an encounter gave you feelings of love, peace and joy, and resulted in the higher good of all concerned, an angel was probably involved no matter how you experienced it. If you felt fear, doubt or confusion, and the encounter created trouble or discord in your life, it probably wasn't angelic in nature.

Angel experts say the celestial beings use the mode of communication that best suits their purpose and our ability to accept the message. Since angels are the messengers and not the message, they don't like to draw undue attention to themselves. Their messages frequently come to us in ways we consider normal and explainable such as through a dream, an inspired thought, or another person who appears at just the right time to offer assistance or inspiration. Thus, sightings of classical angels with all the bells and whistles are quite uncommon.

For some of us, myself included, a dramatic angel manifestation may be too shocking. As much as I love and believe in God's angels, I don't know if I'm ready for the "vision thing." For me, that would be a case of the messenger getting in the way of the message. For now, I'm completely content with the gentle way the angels shower God's blessings on me: the little thoughts that won't go away, the subtle promptings to call someone or go somewhere, the people I "just happen" to meet that turn out to be a great benefit to my life. It's important to honor the subtle ways angels work with us.

There is no way you can force an angel to appear to you, but with faith and prayer, you can invite the angels to help you out in quiet ways. Soon you may begin to feel their gentle nudgings and see evidence of blessings all around.

## Working with the Angels

A word about those subtle inner promptings: Be careful. If you hear a little voice telling you to buy a lottery ticket, it probably isn't an angel speaking. Tuning in to angelic guidance isn't an exact science. It takes some practice. Don't rush out and quit your job, file for divorce or buy a red sports car because you think the angels told you to do so.

And for heaven's sake, don't try something dangerous or foolish just to see if your angel will show up to save you. It doesn't work that way. One local spiritual leader says angels are great respecters of our God-given free will. If we knowingly and willingly put ourselves in harm's way, we limit the angels' ability to help.

If you want to work with the angels, start with something small. Ask them to bless you with patience in a stressful situation, or even to help you find your misplaced keys or some other lost object. When you receive your blessing, no matter how small, take a moment to experience how it felt and to thank God and the angels. As the small experiences start to add up, you'll learn to distinguish between angelic promptings and your own inner voice.

Also, remember that God and the angels are there to help, guide and protect us, but we have to do our part, too. I knew a woman who wanted to rent a room in her house. She prayed about it, but didn't put a sign in front of her house or an ad in the newspaper. She believed the perfect boarder would just appear on her doorstep. She may still be waiting.

Working with the angels is a little like riding a bicycle. If you don't put in any effort, you won't get very far. If you pedal, a bike can help you get just about anywhere you want to go.

When you make a real effort toward your goal, you give the angels more material to work with, more opportunities to be of assistance. Pitch in and do your part. Then ask the angels for help. You'll find for every seed of effort you sow, you'll reap a bushel of reward.

In general, when you call on the angels, use common sense and sincere prayers for guidance. God and the angels will take care of the rest.

## How to Spot an Angel

There are a number of similarities in stories of angelic visitations. Some of the attributes common to many angelic experiences are listed below.

*Peace*. Angels engender feelings of peace and a deep sense of knowing that everything will be all right. An absence of fear in a frightening, anxious or trying situation can also signal angels at work.

*Light*. Some describe angels as pure, white light, more dazzling than any found on earth. Golden or pink hues are also reported.

*Love*. Angels love us like no one on earth. Those who experience angels may say they felt deeply loved and cared for by these celestial beings.

*Happiness, laughter, joy, giddiness*. According to G.K. Chesterton angels can fly because they take themselves lightly.

*Appearance to children*. It seems children are especially open to the angelic realm and are more likely than adults to experience an angel.

*Sweet smells.* The scent of roses or other delicate blossoms may indicate the presence of angels.

*Softness.* Some people say they've felt enveloped in something as soft as down. The reference may be to Psalm 91:4 "He shall cover thee with his feathers and under his wings shalt thou trust."

*Absence of catastrophe, especially on the road.* Sometimes angels bend the laws of nature on our account. When someone can't explain why the car didn't crash when a crash seemed inevitable, angels are often the explanation.

*Memorable.* Angel encounters are remembered vividly. They often stay with a person for a lifetime.

*Form.* Angels have been perceived in human form, as birds or animals, as a disembodied voice, as music or light. Sometimes their actions—those fortunate coincidences—are the only indication of angelic activity.

*Chills.* Some people get a shiver running down their spine when they experience a brush with an angel.

*The messages.* In one way or another, angels often tell us to "Fear not," and "Praise God always."

*Quick and quiet.* When an angel takes a human form, it usually says very little, does its act of kindess, and then, like the Lone Ranger, disappears, often before one can say thank you.

## Answers from the Angels

The publisher of the New Age journal "These Celestial Times," Kathleen Krzywicki had a channeling session—a kind of psychic reading—before publishing an edition of her newsletter entirely devoted to angels (vol. 2, no. 2). She said the Archangel Gabriel came to the session to talk about angels. Krzywicki shared some of the insights she received from the archangel in her article, "Angels Tapping on My Shoulder." Included was the following information which, despite what you may think about channeling sessions, seems as good an explanation as any for why angels' visits are so brief and why they come at all:

Q. When you manifest, how long can you stay on this plane?

A. "We can only evolve for a short time on the earth plane because of the poisons, toxins and the dimness of light. It does not make us less than we are to stay, it weakens us. In the weakness we cannot do our mission work because of the lack of energy. We are pure energy that has never had to evolve in a physical being or form . . ."

Q. When would an angel manifest?

A. "We do not have to come back to earth, but will certainly, when there is a need. One of our main missions is to come back to earth in crossfire moments; moments of extreme emergency or life and death situations. Or, if we see a good soul heading down a bad path because the soul is making bad choices which it doesn't have to. We can step in and intercept."

For he shall give his angels
charge over thee,
to keep thee in all thy ways.

Psalms 91:11

# The Angel Stories

MORE THAN 200 people turned out for a panel discussion on angels and spirits at Landmark Center in St. Paul one frigid February evening in 1993. My sister, Ann, and I were among them. Susan Douglas, one of the panelists, related the following experience.

"I had a wonderful Irish grandma. She married late in life and for many years, there were no babies. So she went to the priest and he said, 'You must paint angels above your bed.' And she did. She hired a local painter who painted angels on the ceiling above her bed. Then she had three daughters.

"I married young, but seven years later, I still didn't have any babies. Then I remembered the story of my grandmother and the angels. I found a picture of a cherub that had been painted years ago by someone in the family. I put it by my headboard. And I had three daughters."

My sister and I looked at each other knowingly. "Toni should be pregnant any time now," she said.

Our brother and sister-in-law had been trying to have a baby for more than a year, with no success. The previous Christmas, Ann had given them a watercolor she'd painted of an angel holding a baby. They'd hung it near their bed. Two days later, David and Toni called with joyous news. The baby was due in October.

J.N.

*"Angel Taking Nibbles to Heaven,"* India ink, Nancy Waller.

In the early 1960s, when I was a child growing up in St. Paul, I was playing with a friend in the backyard of my Marshall Avenue home, between Dale Street and St. Albans. It was a sunny afternoon with blue skies and puffy clouds. As we were playing, a small truck drove down the alley. My pet cat ran out in front of it and was struck dead.

My friend and I went to look at it and we felt so sad. I said, "Let's pray that God will take it to heaven." So, we knelt down together about 10 feet away and prayed out loud. I looked up to see if our prayers were being answered and I saw the angel. It floated down toward the dead cat with its arms reaching out.

It was beautiful, radiant and transparent. It had golden hair—wavy and above the shoulders—and wore a long white robe. I couldn't tell if it was male or female. I had always thought angels had wings, but there were none on this one. It seemed to float down on a ray of sunshine. Though its feet never touched the ground, it gently picked up the cat and then disappeared. After that my friend and I got up to look and could not see the cat anywhere. So we just thanked God for answering our prayer. I told my mother that our cat went to heaven.

Children have an innocence and purity about them. Perhaps that's why God allows them to see what others can't.

*Susan,* Coon Rapids

When my son, Micah, was four years old, we went to a gathering at the Minneapolis Auditorium called the Conference on the Holy Spirit. It began with lots of singing.

At one point, Micah started jumping up and down, pointing and saying, "Mama, Mama. Look at the angels." I looked where he was pointing, but I didn't see anything. I could see a look of frustration in his face. He was clearly upset that I didn't see them. He said, "But they are right there. Two of them. They're dancing." He said they had wings and were wearing long, white robes as they danced above the crowd, enjoying the music.

*Diane Gonzalez,* Minneapolis

I was living in Los Angeles and working at a large children's hospital in a high crime section of the city. I often went outside on my lunch hour to enjoy the sunshine and warm weather. The sidewalks were packed with people, shoulder to shoulder.

One day, a man walking behind me said, "I'm going to kill you . . . I'm going to stab you." A quick glance over my shoulder revealed a total stranger who was filled with rage and only inches behind me. I was terrified and wanted to run, but was trapped in the crowd and couldn't get away. The people around me heard him, too, but no one made any move to help. The threats continued as I walked with the flow of the crowd. My mind was racing frantically. . . . Does he have a gun? . . . Does he think I'm somebody else? . . . Should I turn and confront him? . . . Will anyone help me?

I looked up and saw a man ahead of me on the sidewalk with his arm extended toward me. He stood and waited for me as the sea of people parted around him. He was very tall, head and shoulders above the crowd. When I finally reached him, he put his arm around my shoulder and walked with me. The threats stopped and the angry man was lost in the crowd. Though I'd never seen this man before, he told me he was a psychologist and worked at a nearby clinic. He left quickly and I never got his name or saw him again. I'm sure he was an angel. He'd been so far ahead of me, he couldn't have heard what was happening through the roar of the traffic. But he was there for me when I needed him.

*Ann Engel,* Minneapolis

This happened the summer I was eight years old at my parents' house on the lake. It was a bright night with a full moon. The moonlight was shining through my window and into my clothes closet. I was lying in my bed when I heard something in my closet. I turned only my eyes to look.

There in my closet was a woman dressed all in white. Her hair was long, flowing over her gown. She had a glow all around her. She didn't walk, but flowed out of my closet toward me. I was afraid at first, but something about her calmed me. As she drew near, I closed my eyes. She started to wrap me in angel hair—like the silky white decoration for Christmas trees. (My mother kept our Christmas angel hair in the attic and only took it out at Christmas.)

As she wrapped me in a cocoon I went into a deep sleep. I awoke the next morning with no angel hair on me, but a pile of it on the end of my bed. I told my mother and she believed me. Now, many years later, she tells my four children of the experience.

I'm a very godly person and I feel this was a sign from God that he and his angels would always protect me. For the woman was truly an angel of God.

*Sherry Bell,* Randolph

In spring 1949, my husband was injured in an accident and had a brain concussion. He was unconscious and the doctors didn't

*"Blessed Be,"* water media, Anne Mureé Moen.

give him much hope for survival. We had a 3-year-old and I was pregnant with our second child. It was a very difficult time. One day, I was at home doing the ironing and crying uncontrollably. Suddenly, I heard a voice say, "He's going to be all right." And I said, "Are you sure?" And again the voice said, "Yes. He's going to be all right."

I went running to my parents' home nearby crying, "He's going to be all right. An angel told me." After that I collapsed on their couch and slept. When I went to visit my husband the next day, I had a sense of peace and calm because I knew he would recover, even though he seemed no better. It was a long and difficult process, but he did recover and we've had many happy years together.

*Virginia Stone,* Bloomington

(In a separate note, Virginia said she always says thank you to her guardian angel over her right shoulder, because the angelic voice she heard came from the right. Curiously, Emanuel Swedenborg, an 18th century Swedish philosopher and writer who talked with the angels daily for many years, said the angelic messages he received came from over his right shoulder, too. Maybe there's something to the old idea that a good angel perches on the right shoulder, a bad one on the left.)

Throughout my childhood, I was repeatedly beaten, belted and terrorized by my 6-foot-4-inch father. One day, when I was 12, I saw him coming at me with his black belt to attack me. Something happened inside and I just couldn't bear one more beating. In a panic, I ran up the stairway to my bedroom window and threw myself out onto the roof. Struggling to get away from my father's grip, I slipped and fell backwards. I fell about 15 feet from the

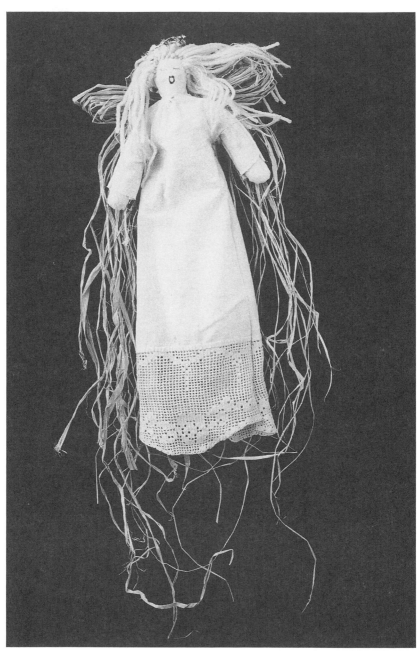

*Angel doll, mixed media, Kristine Warhol.*

second story window. Yet, when I hit the ground, I felt very little impact. In fact, I jumped up and immediately ran two blocks to a church, where I hid out in the choir loft until I felt safe enough to go home. I am certain my guardian angel assisted me in this unbearable situation. I know my angel broke the fall in order to protect me.

*Anonymous*

One summer day, just two weeks after our 12-year-old daughter had died, I was out in the front yard cutting the grass. As I bent down to pull out a weed, I felt a tap on my shoulder. I looked up and saw the profile of a beautiful girl, about 12 or 13 years old. She had blonde hair, like my daughter's. She gave me a bunch of flowers and, before I could even say thank you, she quickly walked away.

I was shocked. I would have dismissed it as my imagination if it hadn't been for the flowers I was holding in my hand. I went inside to show the flowers to my wife. After I told her what had happened, we decided to get into the car and go look for the girl right away. She hadn't been gone long. We drove for blocks and blocks all around the neighborhood, but didn't find her. I'd never seen that girl before and haven't seen her since.

I think she was an angel. God sent her to let us know that our daughter was with him and she was fine. The flowers were a sign of his love. I'd always been a skeptic about this type of thing, but this experience made me a believer.

*Ken Thompson,* Minneapolis

The first Christmas my husband and I were married, we weren't with either of our families for the holidays. I felt sad about that, but we were happy to have each other. One snowy night, very near Christmas, we were driving our Jeep to a friend's house in St. Paul. The Jeep didn't have a radio. We usually talked a lot during those drives, but that night we didn't. We both just sat quietly and watched the snow fall. It was a lonely stretch of highway without another car in sight.

After a while, I began to hear the most beautiful voice singing "Silent Night." It went on for three or four verses. Though I seemed to be hearing it in my head, I know it wasn't my imagination. I don't know the words to even one verse of "Silent Night."

After it was over, I looked at my husband and asked him what he was thinking about. He told me he'd just heard a woman with a beautiful, soprano voice singing "Silent Night."

Sharing that moment, that beautiful experience, was a special gift on our first Christmas together.

*Jean Wright,* Mahtomedi

This happened to my father more than 50 years ago in Wisconsin. He was driving at night, approaching a highway when he saw two cars speeding toward each other in the same lane. They were about to hit head on.

Suddenly, one of the cars was surrounded by angels in flowing white robes. They moved the car into the other lane, out of danger.

*Phyllis Peterson,* Centerville

This happened in 1984 when I was attending William Cary University in Pasadena, California, studying to become a missionary. A friend and her son, who was almost 4 years old, were staying in the dorm with me that weekend.

I was in one bed talking with my friend, who was with her sleeping son in the other bed. He'd been asleep for about half an hour when he woke up very frightened. He was in a panic and kept saying, "They're after me. They're after me." His mother had never seen him so upset before.

I went down the hall to get the director of the dormitory and we all prayed for the little boy. Then we all went back to sleep.

Later that night, I woke up and saw an angel in the corner of the room watching the boy. The angel was so tall he had to crouch down to fit into the room. His wings came around in front of him. He sat on the floor and propped his head in one hand like Rodin's "The Thinker." He was white and luminous. He moved his head toward me, then went back to looking at the boy.

I went back to sleep, but woke up again later. The angel was still there. This time in my head I heard a voice say, "Be at peace. Everything is well." I know I didn't dream this. It really happened.

*Kelly McFarlane,* St. Paul

One summer afternoon the title of a recently published angel book popped into my head and wouldn't go away. I felt like dropping everything to head for the book store. The angels, I was quite sure, were nudging me again.

I wasn't able to get to my neighborhood book store, Odegard Books St. Paul, until about 8 p.m. Once there, I was disappointed to find the book I was after wasn't in stock.

I felt a little silly for thinking there was some fateful reason I

*"Angel with Bass,"* watercolor, Kathleen Priest.

needed to get the book that night. The doubts began. Maybe I was taking all this angelic guidance stuff a bit too seriously.

I picked up another angel book and took it to the checkout counter. There, I happened to glance at a schedule of authors' readings. Jonis Agee, a college writing professor who I hadn't seen in nearly 15 years, was reading that very night at 7:30 p.m. She'd been my favorite professor and a good friend during college. I admire her and her writing tremendously.

Jonis was across the hall at the Music City Cafe, finishing the last few minutes of her reading. Listening to her familiar voice reminded me of how committed she'd always been to her own writing and of how much she'd believed in me. Seeing her renewed my confidence in my own work and in the angels.

After the reading, I visited with Jonis briefly and the point was driven home.

"What were you reading from?" I asked.

"My second novel," she said. "It's called 'Strange Angels.'"

*J.N.*

Once, during a very difficult time in my life, I woke up and saw an angel at the foot of my bed praying for me.

About three months later, during another troubling period, I was making arrangements for leading a shelling expedition. We were to gather seashells on the Mexican Baja. With all the trip preparations, I only had time for an hour's sleep before it was time to go. But I was so tired, I forgot to set the alarm clock. I would have slept through the departure time, if it hadn't been for an angel who awakened me. I was sound asleep and felt myself being hugged awake. I was being embraced with much greater power than that of any human being. I was certain that it was my angel.

*Ruth Reetz,* Bloomington

A woman once told me she and her 8-year-old daughter narrowly escaped a bad car accident. Their car was skidding and they were heading right into some trees. She braced herself, feeling certain they were about to hit a tree, when suddenly the car just stopped. Later, the woman told a friend about this experience as her daughter listened. The woman said she didn't know what kept her from hitting that tree. The daughter said, "Mom, didn't you see the angel? He was standing right in front of the car. He stopped it from hitting the tree."

*Jennifer Johnson,* St. Paul


This happened about 10 years ago, while I was attending mass. It was during the consecration, the part of the mass where the priest lifts the wine and bread up above his head, to be transformed into the Body and Blood of Jesus. When I looked up to watch, I saw angels surrounding the altar, adoring Jesus' presence in the Host. It was a delightful surprise to witness such pure and perfect reverence. Several angels were lying prostrate on the floor, others were suspended in midair around the altar, yet all were at a lower level than Jesus disguised in the Host. They appeared to be 13 or 14 years old, with shoulder-length golden brown hair that shone. They had no wings and neither gender was apparent. They wore beautifully simple long, flowing gowns in heavenly colors: pink, green, yellow, aqua, blue—pale and translucent. Their youthful faces were all focused on Jesus, loving and adoring Him. I was moved by this experience. And I'm so grateful I was granted this privilege that to this day I try to emulate the reverence of these angels during mass at the time of consecration. Even though I saw this only once, I will remember it clearly for the rest of my life.

I know for a fact that angels are present at every mass. I not only believe, I have seen.

*Anonymous*

"Angels, what should I do today?" That's how I've managed the research for this book. Most days I've felt guided in the right direction.

One morning, I got the feeling that I was supposed to go to the Research Center at the Minnesota Historical Society's History Center to look for historical reports of angelic encounters. I resisted, quite sure there wouldn't be much of use to my project in the collection, but the thought wouldn't go away. Begrudgingly, I set off for the History Center. As I started the car, the radio came on playing an Annie Lennox song called, "Precious Little Angel." Laughing, I said, "OK, OK, I believe you. I'm going." As expected, I didn't find what I was looking for at the History Center, but I found something better. One of the staff members took an interest in my project and named several local churches decorated with angels. Even better, his enthusiasm helped me stop doubting the appeal of a book about angel images.

*J.N.*

I was raised Catholic and learned about angels, but I never took them seriously. I never affirmed them as a reality in my own life. But after a number of curious experiences, I started to pay attention to angels.

Because I am a professor of theology, people sometimes tell me strange things. Once, a student from St. Thomas told me that his mother saw an angel hanging on to the top of the car as he drove off to college for the first time. For her it was a reassuring sign that he would be watched over and protected. I wasn't sure how to respond. I hadn't been told anything like that before.

Later, a businessman came up to me after a seminar in Phoenix. He told me he'd gone to the desert alone to do some thinking. A figure in white came up and sat next to him silently. He felt acceptance, affirmation, encouragement. The experience lifted him up and gave him the support he needed. I didn't tell him that his experience seemed rather strange to me.

While researching my book, "The Wisdom of the Celtic Saints," my mentor told me, "When you go to Cornwall, let the angels guide you." And I did. I visited the high places that the Celts associated with angels. That's when I began to take them seriously. I started praying to angels and I began to notice a wonderful synchronicity. Everything seemed to fit together perfectly on that trip.

Back at home, while writing the book, I had another experience that made me believe more strongly in the angels. I'd been writing that day about St. Patrick and how he had had an angel protector named Victor. That same day, I drove to Willmar, Minnesota, to see an old supervisor I hadn't seen in 20 years.

On the way, the car skidded on the ice. Three cars were coming at me at such a speed that they couldn't have stopped. Suddenly, my car swirled around and stopped in the middle of my lane. It just stopped. I've always thought an angel was responsible for that one. If something hadn't intervened, I'm sure I'd be dead. I've come to believe in angels more as these things happened.

Angels are manifestations of God's love and presence. They are there for us whether we recognize them or not.

*Dr. Edward Sellner,* The College of St. Catherine, St. Paul

*"Christmas Angel," wood, plaster and cardboard, James Quentin Young.*

One morning about 30 years ago, I was going to mass at St. Olaf's Catholic Church. I tried to park the car across the street from the church, but I just couldn't get it into the parking space. I tried again and again. "Lord, please help me," I prayed, "I don't want to be late for mass."

A man appeared and offered his assistance. He said, "I haven't driven a car for a long, long time, but I think I could get it parked for you." He was an average-looking man dressed in a white shirt and dark trousers. Normally, I wouldn't let a stranger into my car, but there was something about this person that made me trust him. I opened the door and slid over to the passenger seat so he could get in. He maneuvered the car perfectly into the parking space.

I gathered my things, then turned to thank him, but he was gone. I got out of the car and looked up and down the street. He was nowhere to be seen. One second he was sitting next to me in the car, the next second he was gone.

I'd asked the Lord to help me and he did. He sent my guardian angel.

*Bernie Von Ende,* Golden Valley


I went for a walk on a sunny spring day on Minnehaha Parkway. It was a pivotal time in my life. I was without work and very depressed. While I was walking, I vaguely heard someone shuffling along behind me. I also felt a kind of protective presence, like something was sheltering me. But I was in such a fog of depression that I really didn't pay attention to either of them.

Suddenly, a man came up behind me and put his hands over my face. He threw me to the ground and started to rip my clothes off. I tried to scream, but his hand was firmly over my mouth. I was frightened and angry as I struggled and struggled to get him off me. I finally realized that I couldn't fight him off by myself. I needed help.

Something inside me triggered me to surrender. It was like I walked inside of my head. I felt a presence around me that felt somehow "other" than myself. And I silently said, "I want this man off me. Give me the words."

At that exact moment, his hand slipped off my mouth and I said, "I'm going to tell your mother on you right now." The words just came out of my mouth. I hadn't planned to say that. He jumped off me and ran away. I was so shocked and still so angry, I almost ran after him.

I knew that I had been given a blessing and that my life would never be the same. All I needed to do was to surrrender and trust that angelic, guardian presence around me. If I can do that, I'll be given all I need to know at the time I need it.

During the attack, I knew that no matter what happened to me, I would be OK. I got in touch with that feeling of eternity—the part of me that will never die no matter what happens to my body. That was an invaluable thing. It changed my life.

*Barbara Garland,* Minneapolis


My garage opens onto a very busy alley that adjoins a school parking lot. On school days, cars go speeding through the alley to deliver children to the school door, directly behind my garage.

At the height of the parking lot frenzy, I need to get out of the garage to take my son to daycare. It's like bumper cars out there weekday mornings. I've had countless near accidents that have left me quite shaken.

I tried everything from honking my horn and waving my arms

to calling the school principal. Still tires would screech and horns blare. Nothing helped until I decided to bring in the angels.

Now, before backing out, I ask the angels to clear the way for me. The close calls that once happened at least weekly have now disappeared altogether.

*J.N.*

I was driving down Franklin Avenue in Minneapolis one spring morning with my 4-year-old daughter in the car. I was going to drop her off at daycare before heading to work.

An older man in a big, old car was slowing us down. He was right in front of me, straddling the two eastbound lanes and driving about 20 miles an hour. I couldn't get around him on either side. This went on for blocks and blocks. He was going so slowly, I had to drive in second gear to keep my car from chugging.

Surprisingly, this delay didn't seem to bother me, even though I was in a hurry. Normally, I would have gotten upset, but I figured I couldn't do anything about it, so why be angry?

Finally, the old man turned into a driveway in the middle of the block and disappeared. I looked up and saw the light was still green at the end of the block and accelerated.

Just then, a car came racing out of nowhere and ran the light—which had been red for him for quite a long time. If it hadn't been for the man in that slow-moving old car, we might have been hit in that intersection.

*Ann Engel,* Minneapolis

Our parish pastor's mother had died. When I learned that the church secretary and her husband were going to attend the funeral, which was being held in another state, I asked if I could ride along with them. They were planning to leave at 2 a.m. and would stop by to pick me up.

My two children were little then, and we were living in a two-story townhouse. I asked a woman who lived in the same townhouse project to take care of my children while I was gone. Still, I was concerned about them.

As I sat on the front step, waiting for my ride, I asked God to protect my children all through the night. As I was praying quietly to myself, I suddenly felt a presence behind me. I looked over my shoulder at my front door and saw a magnificent angel standing guard in front of my house. It was suspended off the ground and stood two stories high. He had a huge set of wings, wore a white gown and was surrounded by a radiant white light. A large sword was held upright in his hand, the tip pointing heavenward. He looked to be about 22 years old. Looking at him, I sensed he was strong, protective, good, safe, reliable and definitely from God. As I left my townhouse, I could still see him there protecting my children and my home. God let me know that his angel would not leave until I returned home the next evening. I am indebted to God's angels. They are real and they are here to help us and protect us.

*Anonymous*


Probably the one thing that has kept me the most unhappy in my life has been taking on too much and being overly busy. Once, while I was teaching, I hurried downtown to do some errands on my 24-minute lunch break. As I raced down the sidewalk, an older woman caught my eye. She was the only person I noticed on the crowded sidewalk.

She was walking slowly and lightly. She looked at me with this unhurried, angelic face. I can still see her face. Her body looked like that of an older woman, but her face was young. Her eyes were intensely blue and her face was filled with light. She looked up at me and smiled this heavenly smile and said, "Oh, darling. What's your hurry?" It stunned me and made me reassess my hurried ways. I honestly feel like she was an angel who simply came into physical form to get my attention. Now she can get my attention by reminding me of that day. Even today, when I get too hurried, I see her face.

*Barbara Garland,* Minneapolis

One night I dreamed that my stepmother and I were upstairs in a house. We put out food to attract eagles. One came, but my stepmother couldn't see it because she was in a wheelchair. So I held out my arm and signaled the eagle to come closer. Instead, he came and landed on my outstretched arm. He and I looked at each other deeply and lovingly. I gently drew him in and hugged him. It felt so gorgeous and wonderful. Then I stretched out my arm and he flew off.

It was clear that God sent me a messenger to say, "This lady doesn't get it. She doesn't know how to love or trust. I'll have to tell her in a way she understands." I'm an outdoors person and the eagle means a great deal to me. It's the most powerful connecting messenger of the Great Spirit. So I said, "OK. I believe you. I believe you're out there and that I can trust and feel love, too." After that, whenever I got discouraged, I remembered the eagle.

Since that time, eagles have appeared at auspicious times in my life. During a party we were hosting at our home in Maine, my son told us he and his girlfriend were engaged to be married. A few minutes later, a minister arrived at the party and said, "I've just seen the most amazing thing: An eagle and a raven playing together." While it is rare to see an eagle in that place, it's even more rare to see one cavorting with a raven. To me, it was a blessing for my son and his fiancée. For in some ways, he is a raven and she is an eagle.

Another time, while I was writing the book "Active Older Adults in the YMCA: A Resource Manual," the head of health and fitness for the entire YMCA called to talk about it. As we were on the phone, I saw an eagle in flight outside my window. I had to ask her to hold while I went out to see it. Luckily, she was understanding. I came back on the line and told her that the eagle's appearance must mean the project was blessed. And it was very successful.

I've been in therapy for many years, struggling to overcome the effects of being raised by an alcoholic mother. One day, after a particularly intense session, I drove off, wondering if the breakthrough I'd felt during that session was real or not. Was it just another session or had something very important transpired? I looked for an eagle.

Coming down across the High Bridge in St. Paul, I scanned the Mississippi River. There it was. The eagle made a broad sweep over the river and headed up and over the steep south bank. It flew right up over the neighborhood of the therapist's office and made two big circles before heading downstream where eagles spend the late winter. It was the sign I'd asked for.

I believe God comes to us in whatever form will work for each person. Because I'm an outdoors person who loves birds, eagles are my angels.

*Ann Hooke,* St. Paul

Mine is a family of bird lovers, so it only seemed natural that the angels came to us as birds during a difficult period in our lives. Throughout my father's two-year struggle with brain cancer, birds came to us all to offer healing, courage, hope and understanding.

It all started one tearful April morning. Mom called with the news: Dad had a grand mal seizure the night before. He'd been rushed by ambulance to United Hospital in St. Paul. They didn't know what was wrong. Throughout what was to become my father's lengthy illness, there were only two times that I cried uncontrollably. This was one of them. I tried to pull myself together so I could get to the hospital and be with my parents, but nothing seemed to work.

Just then I looked up and saw a pair of cardinals perched in the bushes just outside the window. A peace came over me and I knew that my parents, like this wonderful pair of birds, would be together for at least a few more seasons. Suddenly I was efficiency itself, calmly canceling appointments for Mom and Dad, calling their priest and alerting a few close friends.

The story of the cardinals calmed Mom and Dad, too, during the first of what would be many hospital stays. A month after the cardinals first appeared, Dad's illness was diagnosed as a malignant brain tumor—a fast-growing and deadly kind. He quickly lost his ability to write and to use numbers. His speech became slurred and difficult to understand.

Cardinals became our symbol of hope and peace, strength and love. They appeared to everyone in the family, just when we needed some encouragement. There were cardinal stickers and greeting cards, cardinal prints on the wall and cardinal ornaments on our Christmas trees. They helped lift us up above the pain and sorrow.

After his first surgery, which removed most of the tumor, a flock of cedar waxwings appeared in the crab apple tree outside Mom's

*"Daedalus," bronze and granite, Brantley Kingman.*

kitchen window. My family has lived in that house for three generations, yet no one ever remembers seeing cedar waxwings in the yard before. They look something like a female cardinal: Crested and grey but marked with a splash of yellow instead of red. We'd learned that the color yellow was associated with the brain and had surrounded Dad with yellow flowers and pillow cases. Now it seemed "yellow cardinals" were coming to offer him strength and healing.

Eight months, and many chemotherapy and radiation treatments later, Dad's tumor began to grow again. His only hope was a difficult surgery that involved implanting radioactive material directly into the tumor. It couldn't cure him, but it could extend and improve the quality of his life. Without the surgery, his life expectancy was measured in weeks. He carefully weighed his options, and decided to have the surgery.

After a grueling surgery and five days in radioactive isolation, Dad was released from the U of M hospital. The procedure had been a difficult, if not torturous one. As Mom drove along Mississippi River Boulevard, heading for home, he turned to her and said, "I feel so weak. Maybe I made the wrong decision."

"No, dear," she answered. "You're going to get your strength back." As she spoke those words, a bald eagle, an unmistakable symbol of strength, soared up out of the river valley and burst out of the woods right in front of their car. From that moment on, there was no doubt in my father's mind that he would regain his strength. And he did. He lived for 14 more months, surprising both his surgeon and oncologist.

During the last months, when he was confined to a wheelchair and could no longer speak, he spent many hours watching the birds at a feeder outside the dining room window. Cardinals, nuthatches, goldfinches, juncos, sparrows and many others mobbed the feeder like never before. Squirrels and rabbits joined in the feasting on the ground, all seemingly for Dad's entertainment.

The birds, which had supported us throughout Dad's illness, came to pay their respects at his burial, too. It was a bright March afternoon, the sun shining in a brilliant blue sky. Mourners gathered in the snow as the priest gave my father a final blessing. The funeral director then presented my mother with an American flag, in honor of Dad's military service. Just as she did so, a flock of black birds (crows? starlings?) shot across the sky right above us. They flew in tight formation, like military jets giving a final salute.

The cardinals, the cedar waxwings, the eagle, and the black birds at the burial acted as angels for my family. They came in difficult times to ease our sorrow, to give us strength and to remind us that God is with us always, even unto death.

*J.N.*

*"Gabriel," oil on canvas, Millie Maria Oden.*

An angel named Mary came to Millie Maria Oden one day and said, "We're so happy that you're going to paint all of us." Over the next seven months, Oden made 14 large oil paintings of angels.

Before each painting, she met with a minister who had psychic abilities. "The angels would appear to him. He described them to me, and I made sketches," she said.

Oden's angels are not for sale, but she does sell photographs of them. She has occasionally shown her paintings at local churches. More often, she displays them in her front yard in Hopkins.

"I put them in a circle. People come over and we have an angel meditation," she said.

Oden told of the two instances when the angel Gabriel appeared to her. The first time, "I was carrying the portrait of Gabriel into the sunlight so I could photograph him. Suddenly I felt the roundness of his body against mine," she said.

Later, Oden reworked Gabriel's face. As the painting dried on an easel in her kitchen, she got a phone call from a friend.

"I was sitting there chatting away on the telephone and looking at the painting. As I'm talking, Gabriel himself appeared. I told my friend, 'Oh my God. Gabriel's here.' I could see his shoulders and head as he stood behind the easel and looked down at his portrait from above. He was over seven feet tall." Oden said the archangel had come this time to let her know that he liked the new face on his portrait.

Oden says people who view her angel paintings often tell her their own stories of encounters with the angels. "Many times they have never told anyone of these events before. They are so afraid that no one will believe them or that people will criticize or ridicule them. But they feel comfortable telling me because they see I've expressed my belief in the reality of angels through these paintings."

You can contact Millie about her work by writing 303 Sixth Ave. N., Hopkins, MN 55343.

One foggy morning around 1980, I picked up my grandmother to take her on some errands. On our way to the grocery store, I stopped at a red light where the street crossed a four-lane highway. When the light turned green, I put my foot on the accelerator and tried to go, but an unusual force prevented me from stepping on the gas. Puzzled, I tried again. Again, my foot was held off the gas pedal for about 15 seconds. I looked up just in time to see a large, speeding car run the red light on the highway in front of us. It was going at least 70 miles per hour and it passed just inches in front of my bumper. I could feel my car rock as the speeding car zoomed by. Then the strange force was gone and I drove my car across the street. Immediately, I knew that my angel had saved our lives by preventing a crash that surely would have been fatal. I thank my guardian angel for it to this day.

*Anonymous*


I'm 78 years old and can't remember what I did last week, but I can remember seeing an angel 51 years ago June 10 as vividly today as the day it happened.

That day we almost lost our first child, Judy, who is now 54. She was 3 years and 2 months old at the time. Judy had gotten sick on a Thursday. The doctor thought it was the flu. Friday she wasn't any better. Saturday morning we met him at the old St. Andrew's Hospital in southeast Minneapolis. Another doctor examined her, took her blood count and said her appendix was ready to burst. He wanted to operate right away.

I didn't feel right about it. I said "no," and called Northwestern Hospital. Dr. Nordland took my call and we brought Judy right over. He knew right away what was wrong. He said her body fluids were very low and they started IVs that morning.

At midnight, they brought her to surgery. My sister, her husband, my husband, Stan, and I were able to go up to the hall right outside the operating room.

I sneaked down the hall, stood against the wall and looked into the room. There was a pure white figure standing next to Dr. Nordland. It was an angel. I started to cry. I knew our child was going to be all right. When I wiped my eyes to look again, it was gone.

We took Judy home after two weeks of around-the-clock nursing care. She was all right.

God had sent one of his angels to be there for our Judy.

*Mrs. Stan Larson,* Minneapolis


Mother often related to me what she experienced when my brother died. Vernon was 5 years old at the time and became ill with scarlet fever which turned into pneumonia. This happened near Park River, North Dakota, in the 1920s, before penicillin.

One afternoon he seemed a little better and mother, encouraged, watched him closely. Soon he fell into a sort of sleep. Then he opened his eyes and, smiling, said, "Oh, look at the angels." Noticing mother's surprise he glanced at her and said, "Can't you see them?" "No," she said, shaking her head. But he again looked up and continued, "They are singing." Quickly he closed his eyes and peacefully died.

Growing up with this family story gave me a great faith in God.

*Rhoda Mead,* Champlin


For the past two years, I have been terribly sick with an incurable disease. I've lost so much weight, I look like a skeleton with skin.

I'm a 33-year-old housewife, I have three children and a wonderful husband. Life has been difficult lately, but we're doing OK. January 25, 1993, is a day I will never forget.

I had been terribly sick. Many dear friends and family members sent me beautiful flowers, plants, crosses, holy water and many other lovely gifts. Many of them had been blessed. I arranged all of them for a photograph. I was lying on the bed and my husband took the picture with his new Polaroid camera and fresh film. He snapped the picture and handed it to me so I could watch it develop.

On the photograph, two little Mexican girls appeared. They were standing on a dirt road with adobe buildings on both sides of the street. They were dirty, poor little girls. Tears welled up in their eyes and ran down their cheeks. Their eyes were so haunting.

The older one had short black hair. Her arm was around the little one's shoulder. The smaller one had long, black hair and was so frightened.

I screamed, "Look! Look!" My husband saw them, too. They were crystal clear images. They made you feel like picking them up to hug them, bathe them, feed them, love them and rock them to sleep. My heart ached to hold them and brush their tears away forever.

Then the picture started to come in. Where the girls once stood, there were now flowers, a cross and the holy water. (The holy water and some other gifts were from Guadalupe, Mexico, where the Virgin miraculously appeared.) I thought it was the film or the camera, so we tried again. And again we had the same results.

I couldn't sleep that night. So I took out my pastels and drew the girls I'd seen in the picture. I worked from 2:30 a.m. to 4:15 a.m. to capture their image on paper. Only then could I sleep.

They were angels with a very profound message for me: "Look. Look right in front of you. You have two little girls who desparately need you. No one else could take care of them like you can. You must go on. You must get well and be there for them." It changed my attitude completely. They gave me the will to go on. And I thank the Lord deeply for their brief visit. I'm slowly getting better now.

*Jean Grimes,* Forest Lake

After eating dinner on New Year's Day 1993, my boyfriend (now my husband) and I were walking arm-in-arm through the poorly lit parking area behind the restaurant. I was looking up at Jeff (he's six-and-a-half-feet tall) as we walked and wasn't watching where I was going.

Suddenly, it felt as if I'd stumbled for a step or lost my stride, but my feet hadn't touched the ground. Then my feet were back on solid ground, and I was walking and laughing with Jeff again. His mouth, however, was wide open and his eyes were round, like saucers.

"You just disappeared," he said. "I was looking into your eyes, then you weren't there, then you were there again."

We stopped and looked back. Not 10 feet behind us was a gaping pothole, maybe three or four feet wide and two or three feet deep. It had been directly in my path—there's no way I could have avoided it. I'd walked right over it, but hadn't fallen in.

Jeff swore I vanished for a second. It surprised me at the time, but it made sense, the more I thought about it. The angels had guided me through another tight spot. My guardian angel was looking out for me, as she had near that same area about eight years ago.

At that time, I was living in Houston, Texas. I was driving home

*Untitled, oil on canvas, Erica Spitzer Rasmussen.*

one night in the pouring rain. It was about 10 p.m., and I was driving on Interstate 59 East with cars in the lanes on my right and left. Coming over a hill, I saw that five cars had just collided about a half mile up ahead.

The car on my left hit the brakes and lost control. He spun around a couple of times and looked as if he was going to crash right into me. Instead, he crossed in front of me and slammed into the pile-up of cars. Then the car on my right joined the crash, too.

I avoided the accident, which was pretty miraculous—but it could happen. What made me believe angels were with me was that I never felt any fear or rush of adrenaline. That amazed me. I never felt any concern. I had a feeling everything was going to be all right. I felt the angels had guided me through it.

After that, I drove home. I intended to go right back out and pick up some groceries. Instead, I looked at a magazine and just fiddled around the apartment. I suppose I detained myself by 10 or 15 minutes before I finally left. As I walked into the grocery store, the police drove up. Shattered glass was everywhere—I'd missed an armed robbery by a matter of minutes.

I've always thought angels were around, but those two incidents in one night woke me up to the fact that angels existed and that I had a guardian angel looking out for me.

*Dawn Holley,* Minneapolis


Most mothers know that children are protected by guardian angels, even before birth. Pregnant women often feel extra angels around them, keeping them and their babies safe. I know I did.

When I was about seven months pregnant, I was driving to a client's office, deep in thought about the project we were going to discuss. Suddenly, I noticed that I was seeing the back sides of road signs. With a start, I realized I'd been driving east in the west-bound lane of a divided roadway for about a quarter mile. I quickly got myself turned around.

Amazingly, there were no other cars traveling in either direction while I was driving the wrong way on that one-way street. As soon as I was safely in the correct lane, the street was filled with traffic going in both directions.

*J.N.*

My first experience with angels occurred when I was relatively young. I was staying with my grandmother in Indiana and attending summer activities at the local elementary school. The day's activities included song and dance practice, which was difficult for me because I was chronically shy.

One day, my group began to practice its own version of "He's Got the Whole World in His Hands." I was reluctant to join the others on stage as they held hands and danced in circles. When I did, I experienced an intense joy in the song. Still, I blushed from bashfulness.

Looking up at the ceiling, I saw a religious mosaic. I noticed what seemed to be flimsy but very real pieces of white cloth extending from the mosaic at several places. Gazing steadily at the mosaic, I realized these weren't just pieces of cloth, but parts of the angels' garments.

Yes, angels were present at our practice. Though our song sounded mediocre to me, it must have sounded grand to the Heavenly Father and his angels.

I left that day knowing that God cared for me enough to allow me this vision of his heavenly host.

*Lageris Veign,* Laporte, Minn.

*"Gladys: Angel of Parking,"* mixed media, Dawn Holley.

Three little miracles:

1. After looking at the angels in the stained glass window at a Minneapolis church, I hopped into the car, turned the key and heard
   these song lyrics over the radio: "Turn your angel eyes my way."

2. I'm not a Bible scholar. In fact, I've never read the good book
   from cover to cover. So many of the passages I found written
   in stained glass stumped me completely. I had no idea where
   to begin looking for them. I can't count the number of times
   I opened the Bible to the very page where the passage I was
   seeking was located. Thanks, angels.

3. I had a few extra minutes while in downtown Minneapolis on
   another project so I drove to Westminster Presbyterian Church.
   Someone had told me there were some good angels inside.
   There was a parking place right in front of the church, but I
   didn't have any quarters for the meter. I said "Sorry, angels.
   If you want me to see this church today, I'll need a meter with
   some time left on it." I pulled out into traffic and, much to
   my amazement, saw another open parking space just ahead of
   me. It had 20 minutes left on the meter.

*J.N.*

This happened when I was a boy, between 5 and 8 years old, living in Willmar, Minnesota. I'd been sick for a few days with a
fever. I woke up early one morning when it was still dark outside
and saw a light coming through the west-facing window near the
foot of my bed. Car headlights often shone through that window
and, at first, this looked like any car lights.

It got brighter and brighter and then a figure—all light—

entered the room silently. There was no noise, no fear. I don't remember seeing any face or arms or feet. Just a figure in light. The whole room was lit up.

It just stood there a few seconds. It turned toward the crib where my little sister slept and then back toward me. It moved over to another bed in the room and stood there for awhile and then moved down the hall to the other bedroom. It stood in the hall outside that bedroom door and, as dawn broke and it got lighter, I saw the figure less and less until it was gone. It didn't disappear all at once, but just faded away.

A case of high fever? Sure. But I was sick a lot in those years and never before or after have I seen anything like that.

*James Nelson,* Beaumont, Texas

One day when I was 4 or 5 years old, I went for a car ride with my mother, her friend and my brother and sister. We were the type of family who always buckled up our seat belts whenever we got into the car.

I was sitting in the back seat looking out the car window at some trees along the road when I heard a voice say, "You're going to be in an accident. You need to take your seat belt off." I trusted that voice. I somehow knew it was my guardian angel. So I took off my seat belt.

Mom continued driving. As she came around a bend, there was a car parked on one side of the road and a group of children picking blackberries on the other. There was no room for our car to get by without hitting either the other car or the children. We slammed into the parked car.

I slid off the seat, hit the seat in front of me and fell to the floor, unhurt. On impact, the windshield shattered into thousands of pieces and broken glass flew into the back seat where I had been sitting.

When a man came to inspect the crash, he said this was one of those rare instances when not wearing a seat belt probably saved me from being injured. If I would have been wearing a seat belt, he said the broken glass would have flown into my face. I could have been blinded.

I've been very sensitive to these kinds of messages all my life. I know that God is always with me so I never have to worry.

*Eva Dyal,* St. Paul

I was terribly afraid of the dark when I was a little girl. I'd start getting frightened before bedtime. Then, lying in bed at night, I'd hyperventilate and shake uncontrollably. I remember crawling into my mother's bed and asking her, "Can little girls have heart attacks?" One night when I was about 4 years old, the fear and shaking started as usual. Then I saw something in the corner of my room. I sat up and saw a small figure, the size of a child, glowing in the dark. At first I was scared, but then a feeling of peacefulness came over me and I fell asleep. It was the first night in weeks I'd had a good night's sleep.

The figure came back again the next night, and the next. It just stood in the corner of my room. I started waiting for it to appear each night. After about a month, when the shaking had stopped and I was no longer afraid of the dark, the figure stopped coming. When I told my mother about the figure, she said it was probably my guardian angel.

*Joy Quam,* Minneapolis

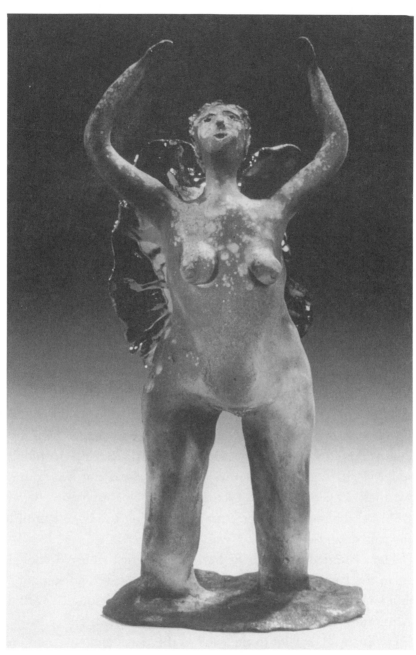

*"Exaltation Angel," raku-fired ceramic, Lou Ann Lewis.*

155

I grew up on a farm in Iowa. For a time, my father drove a frozen meat truck.

One hot summer day when I was 11 years old, I went out to the garage to talk with Dad. The truck's big freezer door was ajar as he took inventory. It was 90 degrees in the shade that day and we didn't have air conditioning in the house. I stepped inside the back of the truck and it felt so cool and wonderful.

The next day I went down to the garage again and cooled off in the truck while Dad was in the yard. He walked over to the truck and told me, "If you're going to go in there you can't leave the door open like that." He showed me how to open the door from the inside. You had to push a bolt forward and then turn it.

The following day it was still hot. I walked the 30 or 40 feet from the house to the garage and got inside the truck to cool off. I was wearing a pair of shorts and a light summer shirt and the cold air felt refreshing against my skin. When it was time to come out, I tried the door, but it wouldn't open. I kept doing what Dad had showed me, pushing the bolt forward and turning it, again and again. The door would not unlatch.

I started to panic. I picked up an empty wooden box, ran the length of the truck and hit the door with it. Still the door wouldn't budge. I checked the hinges to see if there was any way to get the doors off. There wasn't. I screamed for help, but no one heard me. I kept running and screaming and trying to get out until I was hoarse and exhausted. I was trapped.

Then I started to feel light headed. The first time I'd cooled off in the back of the truck, I'd asked Dad how long someone could survive inside. He said you'd start to lose consciousness within 30 minutes. I didn't know how much time I had left.

Giving up, I walked to the back of the truck and sat down on some boxes. The coldness of the wood was far from pleasant on my bare legs. I said, "Lord, you can take me to heaven now. I've done something very foolish."

Instantly there were two big, bright lights on either side of me. They were forms made entirely of light. They were so tall they almost reached to the top of the truck. I could sense their loving, benevolent presence.

They lifted me from under the elbows and we glided toward the front of the truck. I don't remember walking. Then the door just opened—I didn't even touch it. The next thing I knew I was standing outside in the warm sunshine.

They were angels. And they saved my life.

*Tami Kriens,* Mahtomedi

*Detail, "Spring Angel," watercolor, Ann Engel.*

# PART III: Angel Emporium

*Angel mobiles, Gaviidae Common.*

# ANGELIC ETCETERA

E T C E T E R A: unspecified things of the same class. That's as good
a definition as any of the following angel items, bits and pieces
of angel information I gathered along the way.

## ADVERTISING ANGELS

Each holiday season since 1958, CME-KHBB Advertising (formerly
Campbell Mithun-Esty), Minneapolis, has commissioned the creation of angel sculptures to give friends and clients. The gift angels
pay homage to the angels of old, the original great communicators,
and represent the agency's desire to serve as a "sensitive, honest
and productive communicator." Created in a limited quantity by
a different artist each year, the angels originate from all over the
world—Europe, the Middle East and the United States.

## HOLIDAY ANGELS

Eight mobiles graced with 42 neoclassical angels and cherubs have
decorated the Saks Fifth Avenue wing of Gaviidae Common in
downtown Minneapolis for the past few holiday seasons. Designer
and angel collector Robin Mooney created the concept and design;

F.B. Fogg crafted the pastel angels of handmade paper; Smith and Stavig Design worked with Mooney on the project.

### BE AN ANGEL DAY

The first annual Be an Angel Day was Sunday, August 22, 1993. Participants in the non-denominational angel celebration were encouraged to "be an angel. Do one small act of service for someone. Be a blessing in someone's life."

Jane Howard, author of "Commune with the Angels," proposed the idea; the angels she communes with selected the date. Howard suggests hosting an angel party on the next Be an Angel Day. Do a group prayer or meditation inviting the angels to inspire you with ideas of ways you can be of service to others.

For more information on Be an Angel Day, contact Jane Howard, Angel Heights, P.O. Box 95, Upperco, MD 21155. (410) 833-6912.

### MORE ANGEL DAYS

The Catholic church has two special feast days for angels. The Archangels Michael, Gabriel and Raphael are honored September 29. October 2 is the feast of all angels, which honors guardian angels.

### THE ALL-ANGEL HOLIDAY SALE

Christmas needs more angels. Why not raise some funds for your church or a worthwhile cause with an All-Angel Holiday Sale? Sell angel-shaped cookies and angel food cake, angel costumes for family Christmas pageants, angel earrings and pins, angel paintings, angel dolls, angel bookmarks, angel notecards, angel tree toppers and ornaments of all kinds, angel rubber stamps and stickers, angel night lights, booklets of angelic songs, baby T-shirts printed with "Daddy's (or Mommy's) little angel," and whatever else inspires you.

ANGEL PRAYERS FOR CHILDREN

Angel of God my guardian dear, to whom God's love entrusts me here. Ever this day, be at my side, to light, to guard, to rule and guide. Amen.

Matthew, Mark, Luke and John, bless the bed that I lie on. Four corners to my bed, four angels round my head. One to watch and one to pray and two to bear my soul away.

PUT AN ANGEL TO WORK

Sometimes angels appear unbidden to help in times of crisis. At other times, they have to be asked. One local spiritual teacher calls angels "the great unemployed," ready and willing to offer assistance, but waiting for someone to ask. He suggests that whenever you see someone in need, say, "God, send an angel." When you hear a police, fire or ambulance siren, send angels along, simply by saying "God, send angels to everyone involved." Ask God to send legions of angels to heal the difficulties in our families, communities, nation and the world.

ANGEL CLASSES

Check the religion section of the newspaper around the holidays for classes and lectures on angels. Many different denominations offer them.

ANGEL SEMINARS

Peggy McGinley and Jennifer Johnson have been offering angel workshops for several years. The one I attended focused on information about angels and exercises to contact the angels, rather than the swapping of angel stories. Peggy led us in many of the guided meditation exercises in the popular book, "Ask Your Angel." With incense, soft music, an angel slide show and lots of candles and decorative angels, the workshop has a meditative feel. For information, contact Peggy McGinley, 111 Kellogg Blvd. E. #2512, St. Paul, MN 55101.

## CONTACTING THE ANGELS

Barbara Garland has been putting people in touch with their angels through body work for more than 20 years. She starts with a prayer, asking the angels to be present and offer their guidance.

Unlike a psychic reading, where a person with intuitive insight gives a client information they receive from "spirit," Barbara helps clients find their own answers—with angelic help. As she asks questions, she gently touches various areas on the body that somehow help the angels deliver their messages. The client responds with the first thing that pops into one's head—a word, an image, a feeling.

This is definitely not for skeptics, but it does work. The physical component made me a believer. At one point during my session, a great broken-hearted sadness wracked my body. With Barbara's help, I asked the angels to help me understand and release the pain. Immediately, it was gone. I've never felt anything like it.

Barbara also calls on the angels to help groups of people—including business professionals—learn to work together more effectively and harmoniously through "intuitive management," a process that helps people tap into their own intuitive guidance.

Contact Barbara Garland at 2510 W. 39th St., Minneapolis, MN 55410.

## TEN WAYS TO ATTRACT ANGELS

Volumes have been written on how to connect with the angels. Two good books full of angel meditations and specific methods for contacting angels are "Commune with the Angels," by Jane

Howard, and "Ask Your Angels," by Daniel, Wyllie and Ramer. Personally, I do things the old fashioned way: I pray.

Following are a few simple suggestions for bringing more of the angels' light and love into your life. These suggestions aren't guaranteed to produce a spectacular angel encounter. No one can do that. God and the angels decide when and to whom they appear. But these activities can help you tune into the gentle, loving presence of the angels in your everyday life.

1. Pray. (Talk to God and the angels.)

2. Meditate. (Listen to God and the angels.)

3. Thank God and the angels for their continuing help in your life.

4. Paint, draw, sculpt, sew or otherwise create an angel. (It helps if you do steps one through three before you begin. Try creating angels in a group.)

5. Sing angel songs or play heavenly music.

6. Place images of angels in your home.

7. Decorate your home with fresh flowers.

8. Laugh.

9. Perform acts of kindness for others anonymously.

10. Be in nature.

# ANGEL SHOPPING

I THINK IT'S important to have a representation of an angel in the home as a tangible reminder of the work and presence of the real angels in our lives. It doesn't have to be large, elaborate or expensive, but it should be something you feel drawn to personally. From all the resources listed below, you'll be sure to find an angel that's just right for you.

## Angelic Stores

At Christmas and Valentine's Day angels can be found in stores everywhere. The following shops carry angel items throughout the year. I've noted the angel items I found at these shops. Because inventory changes rapidly, you may find a different selection when you visit these stores.

## THE BIBELOT SHOP
2276 Como Ave., St. Paul; 646-5651
1082 Grand Ave., St. Paul; 222-0321

Owner Roxanne Freese has carried angels for years, long before the current angel trend. Recently, I found angel night shirts, jewelry, country art angels, plaster castings of angels to hang on the wall and much more. Near the holidays, angel ornaments and decorations abound. The first angels in my collection came from The Bibelot Shop.

## CELEBRATION DESIGNS:
## GALLERY OF SACRED ART AND CRAFTS
1089 Grand Ave., St. Paul
224-6097

This shop features angel jewelry, greeting cards (some by Tomie de Paola), and artworks of every kind, from handmade paper angels to bronze angel wall hangings, to etchings and sculpture. Calligraphed on handmade paper and framed is the Bible verse, "Be not forgetful to entertain strangers for thereby some have entertained angels unawares." Angels of every style and price range can be found at Celebration Designs.

## THE CRAFT CONNECTION GALLERY
1692 Grand Ave., St. Paul
699-3439

Ceramic angels by Lou Ann Lewis and angel dolls by Mickey Allison are among the items featured at this gallery, a project of the Minnesota Craft Council.

## THE CHERUB'S COVE
307 S. Division St., Northfield
(507) 645-6693

It's worth the drive to Northfield to visit this beautiful shop full
of angels. Angelic items include framed art prints, clocks, stationery, books, reproduction Tiffany stained glass panels, and
jewelry all gracefully displayed among Victorian antiques.

## GRANDE VICTORIA GARDENS
818 Grand Ave., St. Paul
228-0228

Just down the street from Victoria Crossing, this floral and gift
shop features decorative items for the home and garden including
knee-high cast concrete angels for your garden and a plaque featuring a pair of cherubic faces. Several of the Victorian-inspired pieces
are embellished with angels.

## THE PRESENTS OF ANGELS
4404 France Ave. S., Minneapolis
926-8008

Co-owners Kathryn C. Flanagan and Cynthia Reynolds asked
the angels for help in creating this all-angel gift shop and the
results are heavenly. The Presents of Angels is brimming with
angel books, art, crafts and gifts including a section of "Minnesota Angels" produced by local artists and craftspeople.

## SAINT PATRICK'S GUILD

1554 Randolph Ave., St. Paul; 690-1506
Mall of America; 858-9233
754 W. 66th St., Minneapolis; 861-2889
8060 Brooklyn Blvd., Brooklyn Park; 424-8859

Among its stock of religious items, Saint Patrick's Guild has guardian angel pins, a small selection of angel books including one for children, Archangel Michael holy cards and reproductions of several famous icon paintings of angels.

## JUDITH McGRANN & FRIENDS

3018 W. 50th St., Minneapolis
922-2971

The day I visited this delightful shop, the stock of angels included small ceramic cherub ornaments made in Guatemala and large varnished tin angels hand crafted by Rhode Island artist John Reynolds. The tin angels, made by a process called repoussé, are embellished with gold or copper leaf.

ANTIQUE STORES of all kinds are great places to find angels. Many will take your name and the items you're interested in and give you a call if they find such a treasure. The shop listed below is worth special mention.

## ARCHITECTURAL ANTIQUES
801 Washington Ave. N., Minneapolis
332-8344

Stop in to see if the store has any angels in their stock of architectural elements salvaged from older buildings and churches. When I called, angel items included stained glass windows, paintings of cherubs from a chapel in northern Minnesota, and some plaster cherub faces.

# ANGEL ARTISTS

IN ONE WAY or another, all of the following local artists were inspired to create angels. Curiously, most began exploring angelic imagery at about the same time: the early 1990s. Work by these artists is included in this book. (See page numbers in parentheses.) If you'd like to purchase or commission a work of angel art, contact the artist at the address listed below.

*Ann Engel* (pages 8, 19, 27, 53, 103, 159) paints watercolor angels. On a Sunday afternoon during the fall of 1992, Ann read "A Book of Angels" by Sophy Burnham and listened to Alessandro Scarlatti's orchestral and choral work, "Messa di Santa Cecilia." "This combination was incredibly inspiring and served to ignite an artistic and spiritual energy. I've been painting angels ever since." Ann continues to be inspired by classical music and her own angel, who encourages her to paint simply, keeping works light and colorful. She also crafts delightful "spirit dolls," and adorns them with vintage fabric and jewelry. Ann, whose last name happens to be the German word for angel, has a bachelor's degree in art. Color prints of several of her works are available. For information, write Ann Engel, c/o Wingtip Press, P.O. Box 40414, St. Paul, MN 55104.

*Dawn Holley* (page 151) has been active in the Women's Art Registry of Minnesota (WARM) for several years, serving as chair of the group's board of directors from 1991 to 1993. Dawn says she believes in angels, friends and children. "I believe in a good joke and a friendly smile. I believe that being nice to others is a wise and wonderful way to life. I sometimes believe my baby has a better grasp on life at three months than I do at 33 years. I believe that when kindness is demonstrated it is contagious. I hope my art portrays my beliefs." Contact Holley in care of Wingtip Press, P.O. Box 40414, St. Paul, MN 55104.


*Brantley Kingman* (page 139) has been casting bronze sculpture since 1974 and began making angels in 1991. "These sculptures come from my own effort to be aware of the angels' guidance. They are tangible reminders of how delicate and ephemeral life is," he says. Kingman believes our true, spiritual selves are, like the angels, perfect and beautiful, but that celestial beauty and perfection can be eroded by the difficulties of daily life here on earth. To contact Kingman about his work, write 647 Bushaway Road, Wayzata, MN 55391.


*Lou Ann Lewis* (page 155) is a psychotherapist who has worked with women for many years. She's heard many stories of abuse, and also of survival and healing. "Hardly any of the women I worked with were free from feelings of shame about their bodies," she says. Her raku-fired ceramic angel sculptures are "my attempt to celebrate ways women can inhabit their bodies and lives in broad, creative ways, freed from the narrow cultural restrictions of what is female." Her angel sculptures evolved from a series of pots she made with sculpted wings. While exploring the history and mythology of angels, she began forming small clay angels to add to the pots. Eventually, the angels grew in size and became free-standing. To contact Lou Ann about her work, write Wingtip Press, P.O. Box 40414, St. Paul, MN 55104.

*Anne Mureé Moen* (page 120) is a visual artist who works in watercolor and mixed media. She began painting angels in the spring of 1993 at the direction of the celestial beings. The angels are healing forces in the artist's life. They have become her healers, teachers and friends. Anne occasionally invites friends—artists and non-artists alike—to her studio to meditate and paint angels. The process has had a healing influence on several of the participants. From these experiences, she's developed classes for non-artists, including a day-long workshop on painting angels. To contact her about her art work or her classes, write 121 Washington Ave. S., Suite 1708, Minneapolis, MN 55401.

In 1990, *Kathleen L. Priest* (page 126) painted a series of angels playing stringed instruments, created with Psalm 150 as their theme. ("Praise him with the blast of the trumpet, praise him with lyre and harp. Praise him with timbrel and dance, praise him with strings and pipe . . .") More recently, Kathleen has taken a more intuitive approach to the angel theme. She spends a lot of time in prayer and meditation. She purposely ignores her more technical side and begins every painting with virtually nothing in mind, allowing intuition to take over. "When I paint and angels appear, I believe that they are inspired by God. I truly believe that angels exist. I have felt their presence," she says. Contact Kathleen about her work by writing 5543 Richmond Curve, Minneapolis, MN 55410.

*Erica Spitzer Rasmussen* (page 148) turns to classical Greek and Hellenistic sculpture and images from the Renaissance and the Baroque eras for inspiration. "Though I live in our modern world, I strive to preserve a touch of the romantic old world vision," she says. Erica started painting winged figures when she met her husband, and also ran off to Greece to study and paint. "These works came from a time in my life when cupid had penetrated my vision, my heart and my soul," says Erica, who is working on her master's degree in painting and drawing at the University of Minnesota. Write 1381 Searle St., St. Paul, MN 55101.

When her favorite cat, Nibbles, died, *Nancy Waller* (page 116) was devastated. She drew the image of an angel taking the cat in its arms to comfort herself in her grief. "The Angel of Companion Animals is not black or white, male or female, but all combined in the essence of unconditional love," she says. Notecards featuring the Nibbles drawing are among the many works available at Nancy's gallery, Wasteland, 314 W. 42nd St., Minneapolis, MN 55409, which is dedicated to the theme of Global Environmental Degradation. Every object on exhibit at the gallery is hand made from recycled materials and is of original design.

*James Quentin Young* (page 131) is an artist and a retired art instructor. He began using religious imagery in his work while studying at the University of the Americas in Mexico City, where he received a master's of fine arts degree in painting. Crafted of wood, cardboard and plaster, his "Christmas Angel" was first exhibited at Word of Peace Lutheran Church, Rogers, Minn., in December 1991. It was part of a Society of Minnesota Sculptors group show at the Lutheran Brotherhood Building in Minneapolis in January 1994. I think it would be a perfect Christmas or year-round embellishment for a church, especially one of modern design. Contact James through the Art Resources Gallery, 494 Jackson St., St. Paul, MN 55101.

# ANGEL CRAFTS

*Dorothy Kenney* was moved to create hand-made angels out of an odd assortment of materials and supplies she found while cleaning out her closet. It became a metaphor for God's love and care for us. "He takes us with what we have and uses all the old broken pieces of our lives to make us beautiful," she says. Kenney makes two sizes of angels from colorful foil paper and smaller angels from white lace. Her business, For Heaven's Sake!, is located in the lower level of 79 Western Ave. N., St. Paul, and is open by appointment. Call 292-0147.

*Ruth Reetz* creates angel ornaments, plaques and night lights from seashells. Called "Angels of the Sea," her works have been twice chosen to be included in the Smithsonian's Christmas tree ornament collection. Ruth also leads shell-collecting expeditions to various seaside locales from the Arctic Circle to the Caribbean. Contact Ruth by writing 40 Norman Ridge Drive, Bloomington, MN 55437.

*Kristine Warhol,* (p. 122) a doll-maker since 1990, has been making angel dolls for more than two years. As reminders of the angels' love, her dolls are especially healing. Each doll is made with antique linens and buttons. They come with cards stating their names, which all begin with the letter "A." "It's my belief these dolls assist in balancing out any negative energy and my hope that they generate love and acceptance of all situations." Brides, new mothers and angel collectors are among those who have bought Kristine's angels. They are available at Bachman's gift shops, Blanc de Blanc of Wayzata, Letter Perfect, Deephaven, and Presents of Angels.

# ANGELS BY MAIL

The following list of angel-related businesses was accurate at the time of publication, but things do tend to change rapidly. Write or call for information before you send money to any of these organizations.

## Publications

ANGELS CAN FLY
This quarterly newsletter is published by Terry Lynn Taylor, best-selling author of the books "Messengers of Light," "Guardians of Hope" and "Answers from the Angels." It includes letters from readers, information on angels, angel conferences and products. Subscriptions are $12 per year. Write Angels Can Fly, 2275 Huntington Dr., #326, San Marino, CA 91108.

ANGEL TIMES
This magazine features stories about angels and the people whose lives they have touched as well as angel art, book reviews and more. Write, call or check your book store for this full-color, glossy magazine. 4360 Chamblee-Dunwoody Rd., Suite 400, Atlanta, GA 30341. (404) 986-9787.

ANGELIC PATHWAYS TO A HIGHER CONSCIOUSNESS
A monthly, New Age newsletter with information related to spiritual growth. Write Pauline Gough, 18110 NW 41st Ave., Ridgefield, WA 98642 for more information.

ANGEL WALK
For information on this New Age newsletter and other publications, write P.O. Box 1027 Riverton, WY 82501

ANGELWATCH
A bi-monthly newsletter for angel enthusiasts, AngelWatch contains reviews of angel books, notices of angel events, information on angels in art, background on specific archangels, stories of angelic visitations and a listing of angel clubs, mail order houses, publications and more. The professional looking and reading newsletter is edited and published by Eileen E. Freeman, author of "Touched by Angels." Perhaps because Freeman holds a doctorate degree in theology from Notre Dame, the publication is especially well-researched and insightful. It's also fun to read. As a clearinghouse for angelic information, AngelWatch is a must for any serious angel buff. Subscriptions are $16 per year. Write P.O. Box 1397, Mountainside, NJ 07092; Call (908) 232-5240, FAX (908) 233-1339.

MAMRE PRESS, INC.
Author and publisher John Ronner maintains an extensive catalog of angel-only books including his own popular and informative books, "Do You Have a Guardian Angel?" and "Know Your Angels." For a catalog, send a self-addressed, stamped, business-size envelope to Mamre Press, 107 S. Second Ave., Murfreesboro, TN 37130.

THE HIGHER CHOICE
Send a self-addressed stamped envelope for more information on this New Age newsletter. Box 65, Nestsu, OR 97364.

THESE CELESTIAL TIMES
This quarterly newsletter covers angels as well as many New Age topics. Subscriptions are $20 per year. Write P.O. Box 8094 Gaithersburg, MD 20898-8094.

## Angel Organizations

ANGEL COLLECTORS' CLUB OF AMERICA
This large club has local chapters, conventions, a quarterly newsletter and more. Annual dues are $12. Write 16342 W. 54th St., Golden, CO 80403.

ANGELS OF THE WORLD
Not just for collectors, this club offers a bimonthly newsletter, a membership pin, conventions and a chance to participate in various angel-related projects with other members. Annual dues are $7. Write 1236 S. Reisner St., Indianapolis, IN 46221.

PHILANGELI (FRIENDS OF THE ANGELS)
A Catholic prayer organization focusing on angels. Write 1115 E. Euclid St., Arlington Hts., IL 60004.

TAPESTRY
This group holds a national conference and other angel-related activities. Tapestry's founder, Karyn Martin-Kuri, paints lovely angel images using watercolors and pastels. She especially likes painting other people's guardian angels. For information about Tapestry or Karyn's angel paintings, write P.O. Box 3032, Waquoit, MA 02536. Call 1-800-28-ANGEL.

## Angel Items

AGNES KRUMINS
Sparkles, crystals or flowers grace these hand-painted cards. Themes include angels and fairies. Custom designs available. For a title list, write 77 Davisville Ave., #1810, Toronto, Canada M4S 1G4.

ANGEL BLESSINGS
Angel cards. Write P.O. Box 28471, San Diego, CA 92198.

ANGEL IMAGES
Lois East paints your personal angel's portrait in pastels. For more information, send a self-addressed, stamped envelope to Lois East, P.O. Box 280843, Lakewood, CO 80228; or call (303) 985-1461.

ANGEL PRODUCTIONS
Tapes and music boxes are among the angel items offered. Write 2219 Desert Creek, Simi Valley, CA 93063.

ANGEL WORLD
Angel jewelry in gold, silver and pewter. Write P.O. Box 210654, Columbia, SC 29210.

ANGELIC ALLIANCE
Jane Howard, author of "Commune with the Angels," and proponent of Be an Angel Day, offers Angelic Attunement Cards, an angel nightshirt and mug. Write P.O. Box 95, Upperco, MD 21155.

ANGELS & THINGS
Write 8236 E. 71 St., Tulsa, OK 74133 for more information.

ANGELS BY THE SEA
Write 75 Mt. Hermon Rd. #C, Scotts Valley, CA 95066. Call (408) 439-0696.

ANGEL'S EXPRESS
Books, notecards, stickers, rubber stamps, picture frames and more from the publisher of "These Celestial Times." For a catalog, write P.O. Box 8094, Gaithersburg, MD 20898-8094.

ANGELS FOR ALL SEASONS
An angel store in Denver now has a spectacular catalog overflowing with marvelous angel items. For a copy, write, 3100 S. Sheridan Blvd., Denver, CO 80227. Call (303) 935-7033.

ANGELS FOR EVERYONE
Chloe Eaton established this home-based business to create angels for one and all. For a catalog, write 27766 Berwick, Mission Viejo, CA 92691.

THE ANGELS' RAINBOW
Angel items are available by writing P.O. Box 1514, Summerland, CA 93067.

CHEERFUL CHERUB
This Catholic family magazine has lots of angel stories and offers rubber stamps and other angel items for sale. Write P.O. Box 26302, San Diego, CA 92196.

CREATIONS BY JOYA
Hand-tinted greeting cards, bookmarks, stationery, post cards and a calendar are offered, some with angel quotes and Bible verses. For a catalog, send $1 to 8441 Flagstone Drive, Tampa, FL 33615.

CREATIVE GIFTS
Heirloom treetop angels handcrafted in Vermont by Susan Strifert for those who cherish the traditions of childhood. Send a self-addressed, stamped, business size envelope to 54 Horizon View Dr., Colchester, VT 05446; (802) 862-0176.

EVERYTHING ANGELS
T-shirts, jewelry, books, notecards and gifts. Send $2 for a catalog, refundable with order. Call 1-800-99-ANGEL, or write P.O. Box 467, New York, NY 10028-0004.

FLAIR GRAPHICS
Finely detailed angel notecards. Six different designs. $10 for 12 cards and envelopes. For a free brochure, write P.O. Box 1028 Sedona, AZ 86336. Call (602) 284-9675.

THE FOOLS JOURNEY
Great angel T-shirts and nightshirts for infants through adults. Write 1900 Vallejo, Suite #201, San Francisco, CA 94123; (415) 567-0951, FAX (415) 346-1252.

HAND AND HAMMER
Beautiful sterling angels inspired by famous works of art and cast by the lost-wax process. Call 1-800-SILVERY for a catalog.

HEART'S DESIRE
Hand-painted angel T-shirts, sweatshirts and denim jackets. Write
4727 Transit Rd., Depew, NY 14045. Call (716) 656-1220.

HEAVENLY SCENTS
Many nice cherubs and angels. Write 5827 Stony Hill Rd., New
Hope, PA 18938.

IntelligenTEES
Angel T-shirts. For a catalog, write 1212½ W. Cary, Richmond,
VA 23220.

JEFFERSON ART STUDIO
These intricately carved porcelain picture transparencies are called
lithophanes. The unusual engravings are made into nightlights,
fairylamps and sun-catchers. "The Guardian Angel" is a best seller.
(My son has one in his room.) Write 4371 Lima Center Road, Ann
Arbor, MI 48103. Call (313) 428-8861.

JEFF STEWART ANTIQUES
Silver angel jewelry. Send $2 for a catalog to P.O. Box 105, Newton,
NC 28658.

ANDY LAKEY
Andy Lakey started painting angels after a brush with death that's
described in Eileen Freeman's book "Touched by Angels." His
abstract angel "outlines" decorate the end pages of her book. To
contact him about his paintings or wearable angel art, write 40485-D
Murrieta Hot Springs Road #335, Murrieta, CA 92563.

## Mariann Loveland

A professional artist who has exhibited her angel paintings in museums, Mariann Loveland paints angels in a wide variety of styles. To contact her about her work, write Mariann Loveland, 444 N. Aurora St., Ithaca, NY 14850.

## Marilynn's Angels

You may have read Marilynn Carlson Webber's angel articles in Guideposts magazine. For a catalog of her angel gift items, send $1 and your name and address to 275 Celeste Dr., Riverside, CA 92507. Write "catalog request" on the outside of the envelope.

## Sandra Martindale

This angel artist paints other people's angels or the angels who "come pose" for her. Write P.O. Box 955, Black Mountain, NC 28711 or call (704) 686-4050.

## Music Design

A deck of of 52 Angel Cards, each with a different design. Pick a card with a specific question in mind for insight into your inner life. Write 4650 N. Port Washington Road, Milwaukee, WI 53212; Call 1-800-862-7232.

## My Little Angel

. . . tells me I'm special. These cuddly angel dolls and audio tapes reassure children that they are special, valued and loved. The tapes consist of a beautiful angel story accompanied by soothing music. Write P.O. Box 70, Hansville, WA 98340. Call 1-800-348-0404.

### OTW PRODUCTIONS
Sally Simonetti hand gilds photographs of her angel paintings and makes them into framable cards. She's committed to painting angels that will raise people's spirits. Write her at OTW Productions, 1541 N. Laurel Ave., #105, Los Angeles, CA 90046-2540.

### RED ROSE COLLECTION
A glossy catalog of New Age inspired clothing, jewelry, books, home decorations and more that includes many angel items. P.O. Box 280140, San Francisco, CA 94128-0140; 1-800-374-5505.

### THE WHISTLING ANGEL
Angel tree ornaments, rubber stamps, cards, rag dolls, wallhangings and more. For a catalog, write 2420 Live Oak, San Angelo, TX 76901; (915) 949-3652.

SOURCES: AngelWatch, These Celestial Times, Angels are Light.

# Bibliography of Sources and Other Angel Readings

Anderson, Joan Wester. "Where Angels Walk." New York: Barton & Brett, 1992.

Attwater, Donald and Thurston, editors. "Butler's Lives of the Saints." New York: P.J. Kennedy & Sons, 1956.

Burnham, Sophy. "A Book of Angels." New York: Ballantine Books, 1990.

Burnham, Sophy. "Angel Letters." New York: Ballantine Books, 1991.

Catholic Biblical Associaton of America. "The New American Bible." New York: P.J. Kennedy & Sons, 1970.

Daniel, Willie and Ramer. "Ask Your Angels." New York: Ballantine Books, 1992.

Davidson, Gustav. "A Dictionary of Angels (Including the Fallen Angels)." New York: The Free Press, 1971.

Duncan, Alastair. "Tiffany Windows." New York: Simon and Schuster, 1980.

Freeman, Eileen Elias. "Touched by Angels." New York: Warner Books, Inc. 1993.

Gilmore, G. Don. "Angels, Angels, Everywhere." New York: Pilgrim Press, 1981.

Godwin, Malcolm. "Angels: An Endangered Species." New York: Simon and Schuster, 1990.

Hansen, Eric C. "The Cathedral of Saint Paul: An Architectural Biography." St. Paul, Minn.: The Cathedral of St. Paul, 1990.

Herberman, Charles G., et al, editors. "The Catholic Encyclopedia." New York: Robert Appleton Company, 1907.

"The Holy Bible." King James Version. New York: Ivy Books.

Howard, Jane M. "Commune with the Angels." Virginia Beach, Virginia: A.R.E. Press, 1992.

Janson, H.W. "History of Art," second edition. New York: Harry N. Abrams, Inc., and Englewood Cliffs, N.J.: Prentice-Hall, Inc., 1978.

Krzywicki, Kathleen, *Angels on My Shoulder,* "These Celestial Times," vol. 2., no. 2.; Spring, 1993. Used with permission.

Lipshultz, Sandra LaWall. "Selected Works, The Minneapolis Institute of Arts." Minneapolis: The Minneapolis Institute of Arts, 1981.

Lloyd, John Gilbert. "Stained Glass in America." Jenkintown, Penn.: Foundation Books, 1963.

Mundale, Susan, editor. "Haven in the Heart of the City: The History of Lakewood Cemetery." Minneapolis: Lakewood Cemetery, 1992.

Ronner, John. "Do You Have a Guardian Angel?" Indialantic, FL: Mamre Press, Inc. 1985.

Ronner, John. "Know Your Angels." Murfreesboro, Tenn.: Mamre Press, 1993.

Taylor, Terry Lynn. "Answers From the Angels." Tiburon, Calif.: H.J. Kramer, Inc., 1993.

Taylor, Terry Lynn. "Guardians of Hope." Tiburon, Calif.: H.J. Kramer, Inc., 1992.

Taylor, Terry Lynn. "Messengers of Light." Tiburon, Calif.: H.J.Kramer, Inc., 1992.

Wall, John. *Church Art and Architecture,* "Church of St. Luke: A Centennial Memoir 1888–1988." Patricia Condon Johnston, editor. St. Paul, Minn.: Church of St. Luke, 1988.

## Photo and Illustration Credits

The author wishes to thank the following organizations and individuals for granting permission to use the images indicated below:

# Index to Angel Sites

*Page numbers of illustrated sites are in italics.*

## About the Author

On Christmas Eve 1992, Joan Nyberg attended midnight mass and said a prayer for more joy in her work. The next morning the idea for a book about angels in the Twin Cities came to her, like a gift left under the tree. Her interest in all things angelic began in the early 1980s and has grown steadily over the years.

She established Joan Nyberg Communications, a free-lance writing business, in 1988, and has written brochures and newsletter articles for many Twin Cities area corporations.

Prior to establishing her own business, Nyberg worked as a publicist and/or staff writer for several Twin Cities organizations including Control Data Corporation, Ellerbe Architects and The Minneapolis Institute of Arts. She has a bachelor's degree in journalism.

## About the Photographer

Many of the photographs in "A Rustling of Wings" were taken by the author's husband, Richard Nyberg. A mechanical engineer with artistic sensibilities, Nyberg resisted the urge to take up photography until 1987, when he delved into the subject with abandon. "I always knew I could lose myself in the technical side of photography," he says, "and I did." Through study and practice, he also developed a fine eye for composition. A project engineer for 3M, Nyberg is a man who takes his hobbies seriously. He is passionate about bicycling, downhill and cross-country skiing and music—particularly jazz.

Angels bring us many blessings, but miracles can come to us in other ways, too. If you have experienced a miracle or a miraculous healing in your life—whether or not an angel was involved—I'd like to hear from you. Please describe the event in a letter to Joan Nyberg, P.O. Box 40414, St. Paul, MN 55104-0414. I will contact you if I'd like to include the experience in a publication.

Order Form

# ·Wingtip·Press·

P.O. Box 40414
St. Paul, MN 55104-0414

Please send me _____ copy (copies) of "A Rustling of Wings:
An Angelic Guide to the Twin Cities," by Joan Nyberg.

For each book, I am enclosing a check or money order for $15.95
(Minnesotans add $1.04 sales tax, St. Paul residents add $1.12 sales tax)
and $3.00 shipping.

Name _____

Address _____

_____

Autograph to _____